Longman Proficiency Practice Exams

Roy Kingsbury and Guy Wellman

Longman Group Limited
*Longman House, Burnt Mill, Harlow,
Essex CM20 2JE, England
and Associated Companies throughout the world.*

© Longman Group UK Limited 1986
All rights reserved. No part of this publication may be reproduced, stored in a retrieval system or transmitted in any form or by any means, electronic, mechanical, photocopying, recording, or otherwise, without the prior permission of the Copyright owner.

First published 1986

Set in 9/11 pt Plantin
Printed in Spain
by TONSA, San Sebastian

ISBN 0-582-55954-5

SPECIAL NOTE ABOUT PAPER 5 INTERVIEW

We have provided in these Practice Exams material which accords with the December 1985 changes in the format of the Paper 5 Interview. Thus, the interview is based on a picture stimulus, related passages for comment, and other material in the form of realia (with perhaps one other activity) – all connected thematically. Please note, however, that in the Cambridge Proficiency examination interview proper, the following conditions apply:

1. The interview may be based partly, and as an option, on one of the prescribed texts.
2. The interview may be conducted with an individual candidate or with a group of two or three candidates.

Acknowledgements

We are grateful to the following for permission to reproduce copyright photographs and artwork:
J. Allan Cash Library for page 70; Central Office of Information for page 35; Josip Ciganovic (Roma) for page 17; Alan McKay for page 13; Research Defense Society for page 53; World Society for the Protection of Animals for page 52.

We are grateful to the following for permission to reproduce copyright material:
Jonathan Cape Ltd for extracts from the jacket of *Hotel Du Lac* by Anita Brookner (1984); Commission for Racial Equality for an extract from the essay 'Race in the Inner City' by John Rex in *Five Views of Multi-Racial Britain* (CRE 1978/1980); J M Dent & Sons Ltd and Walker & Co Inc for an extract from *Earthshock* by Basil Booth & Frank Fitch (first pub J M Dent & Sons Ltd Copyright 1979); The Economist Newspaper Ltd for an extract from the article 'Shadows from the past' p 77 *The Economist* (5/1/85); the author, Sally Emerson for an extract from her article 'Recent Fiction' p 99 *Illustrated London News* (Dec 1984); Headway Publications Ltd for an extract from the article 'Keeping your ideas to yourself' pp 40–41 *Moneycare* (Nat West Magazine Oct 1983) (c) Headway Publications/Moneycare Magazine; the author's agents for an extract from *All Creatures Great and Small* by James Herriot (pub Michael Joseph); Macdonald & Co (Publishers) Ltd for an extract from *Unfinished Journey* by Yehudi Menuhin the author, Norman Myers for an extract from his article 'How the song birds choked on fast food' p 15 *The Guardian* (6/12/84) Copyright Dr Norman Myers, Consultant in Environment and Development, Oxford, UK; Times Newspapers Ltd for an extract from table on p 10 *The Times* (10/12/85) and extracts from the articles 'Safety at work or a safe job?' by David Lipsey p 22 *The Sunday Times* (23/12/84), 'Eyrie of the city falcon' by Tim McGirk p 13 *The Sunday Times* (30/12/84), 'What's in the job for you' p 71 *Sunday Times Magazine* (18/11/84), 'Pains of being a child of gold' by Lewis Chester p 14 *The Sunday Times* (6/1/85), 'How museum 'detectives' unravelled a 2,500 year old murder' *The Sunday Times* (7/10/84), 'School inspectors want grammar at forefront in teaching English' p 3 *The Times* (3/10/84), 'Writing for the screen' by David Section p 41 *The Sunday Times* (16/12/84), 'Curse fails to impress judge' *The Times* (11/2/82).

Contents

Exam One

Paper 1: Reading Comprehension	2
Paper 2: Composition	9
Paper 3: Use of English	10
Paper 4: Listening Comprehension	14
Paper 5: Interview	17

Exam Two

Paper 1: Reading Comprehension	19
Paper 2: Composition	26
Paper 3: Use of English	27
Paper 4: Listening Comprehension	31
Paper 5: Interview	35

Exam Three

Paper 1: Reading Comprehension	37
Paper 2: Composition	44
Paper 3: Use of English	45
Paper 4: Listening Comprehension	49
Paper 5: Interview	52

Exam Four

Paper 1: Reading Comprehension	54
Paper 2: Composition	61
Paper 3: Use of English	62
Paper 4: Listening Comprehension	66
Paper 5: Interview	70

Tapescripts for Paper 4: Listening Comprehension	72

The Key appears as an 8-page pullout section in the middle of the book.

Exam One

PAPER 1: READING COMPREHENSION

Time: 1 hour

This Paper is in two parts, Section A and Section B. For each question you answer correctly in Section A you gain one mark: for each question you answer correctly in Section B you gain two marks. No marks are deducted for wrong answers. Answer all the questions. Indicate your choice of answer in every case on a separate sheet. Follow carefully the instructions about how to record your answers.

Section A

In this Section you must choose the word or phrase which best completes each sentence. For each question, 1 to 25, indicate on your answer sheet the letter A, B, C or D against the number of the question.

1. I hope this headache . . . . soon.
   A goes out   B comes away   C wears off   D passes away

2. What the treasurer said virtually . . . . to a confession.
   A amounted   B came   C stood   D embodied

3. Marrying into such a rich family had always been . . . . his wildest dreams.
   A under   B above   C over   D beyond

4. We failed to lay eyes on a tiger during our expedition, ... film one.
   A let alone   B not to mention   C apart from   D but for

5. The . . . . of the word is unknown, but it is certainly not from any Latin-based language.
   A extract   B derivation   C genesis   D descent

6. Whether the sports club survives is a matter of complete . . . . to me.
   A disinterest   B importance   C indifference   D interest

7. Unsalted butter is best for this recipe, but . . . . that, margarine will do.
   A except   B given   C for all of   D failing

8. Union leaders feel it is time Cabinet Ministers put their . . . . on the table regarding their long-term plans.
   A cards   B hands   C feet   D papers

9. For the first night's performance the . . . . had to be called in to take the part because the leading lady was ill.
   A substitute   B understudy   C reserve   D deputy

10. A peculiarly pointed chin is his most memorable facial . . . .
    A feature   B trait   C mark   D aspect

11. She prides herself . . . . never having had a day off sick.
    A in   B on   C for   D of

12 Just lick the gummed part of the .... and seal the envelope down.
    A slot   B tray   C flap   D frame

13 I .... to think what will become of him now that he has actually been evicted.
    A fear   B loathe   C dislike   D dread

14 The clumsy boy tripped and sent the whole pile of metal plates .... to the ground.
    A clattering   B tinkling   C thudding   D pattering

15 The Headmaster of the local comprehensive school is due to meet his .... in the nearby public school tomorrow.
    A correspondent   B double   C counterpart   D clone

16 Today's activists are .... to pursue one cause to the exclusion of all others.
    A apt   B susceptible   C used   D intent

17 Please find enclosed our .... scale for life insurance premiums.
    A slipping   B sliding   C gauging   D raising

18 Your reluctance to join us so soon after your tragic bereavement is entirely ....
    A comprehensive   B permissible   C comprehensible   D understandable

19 The depleted column was barely able to .... the enemy attack.
    A withstand   B expel   C withhold   D smash

20 According to a hospital spokesman, hopes were .... last night that the unnamed victim would ever regain consciousness.
    A growing   B decreasing   C increasing   D fading

21 In some countries, confrontation between police and strikers on .... has become a feature of life in the eighties.
    A dole queues   B picket lines   C back benches   D assembly lines

22 They were .... tempted to relieve the shopkeeper of his three juiciest-looking apples.
    A badly   B sorely   C powerfully   D utterly

23 The renovation work will .... closing the local library for six months.
    A entail   B result   C ensure   D accomplish

24 His appearance at the reception with the late Mayor's widow caused something of a ....
    A confusion   B rumour   C wonder   D stir

25 Believe it or not, he has even .... to swindling his own friends.
    A reduced   B declined   C sunk   D connived

Section B

In this section you will find after each of the passages a number of questions or unfinished statements about the passage, each with four suggested answers or ways of finishing. You must choose the one which you think fits best. For each question, 26 to 40, **indicate on your answer sheet** *the letter A, B, C or D against the number of the question. Give* **one answer only** *to each question. Read each passage right through before choosing your answers.*

First passage

On 27 January 1950 I was due at the Albert Hall, London, where Sir Adrian Boult was to conduct a programme including the Elgar and the Mendelssohn Violin Concerti. Diana and I left New York on the evening of the twenty-fifth, with ample time, as we presumed, to keep our appointment. With everyone secure in his safety belt, the plane shot down the runway, then halted with a tremendous screeching of brakes just short of takeoff. This was twice repeated before the shaken passengers were unloaded and told to return to the airport in the morning.

Next day we set off for England again. To begin with, so thick was New York traffic that we almost missed the plane, which might have saved everyone a great deal of trouble. Disaster avoided, we took off at eleven-thirty, and shortly afterwards the pilot made his rounds. Wanting to reassure Diana, I stopped him and suggested that the untoward incidents of the day before hadn't been too serious. In that wonderful calm bluff English way, he answered, 'Airplane engines, you see, are made up of thousands of individual parts, and it is quite impossible to tell when any one of them may cease to function'; with which Job's comfort he passed on. A short while later one of those many parts did indeed cease to function: oil began blowing over the wings, and back we went to Idlewild Airport, as it then was. At the third try, later that afternoon, we succeeded in crossing the Atlantic, making one stop to refuel in Newfoundland and another at Shannon in the Irish Republic, for one flew from landfall to landfall in those days.

Here the English weather blocked further progress: fog had closed London Airport. It was about 6:30 a.m. local time when we arrived at Shannon, too early to despair of reaching our destination. We telephoned my agent, Harold Holt, and I borrowed an airport office to practise in. However, as the hours passed and the London fog failed to lift, I grew anxious enough to try to charter from Aer Lingus a plane small enough to land in conditions which our big Stratocruiser could not cope with. For some reason Aer Lingus was not allowed to rescue us, so after more endless hours, we took off in the transatlantic plane, first at three forty-five – when the radio was found to be out of order and we had to turn back, then, finally, at four-fifteen. All hopes of rehearsing had long been abandoned, but the concert itself still seemed safe. The fog had yet a couple of tricks up its sleeve, however. After circling over Heathrow a few times in a vain attempt to find a break in the blanket below him, the pilot landed at Manston on the east coast. Diana and I were delivered to the earth through the luggage shaft in the plane's belly, hustled through customs at a trot and thrust into a waiting car, which roared off the airfield with most gratifying drama. One mile farther on, the gentle fog of the countryside rolled toward us in thick, soft, totally opaque clouds, and we crawled the rest of the way at hardly more than walking speed, Diana shivering in the unheated car.

We were of course late.

26 After the first attempts to take off, the author and his wife were asked to come back on
    A 25th January.
    B 26th January.
    C 27th January.
    D 28th January.

27 The pilot's remarks, shortly after taking off from New York,
    A proved quite inaccurate.
    B led to their returning to Idlewild.
    C referred to their previous disastrous flight.
    D were not calculated to ease Diana's distress.

28 When they arrived in Ireland at 6.30, the author and his wife
    A were still hoping to reach London in time to rehearse.
    B chartered a small plane which could land in fog.
    C were late for their connecting flight.
    D were feeling absolutely desperate.

29 What happened when they finally landed at Manston?
    A They were held up going through Customs.
    B The fog immediately came down thicker than ever.
    C They were given special treatment.
    D Their car developed an engine fault.

30 It is evident from the passage that the author was
    A a rich man taking his wife to see a special concert at the Albert Hall.
    B a conductor who had to be in London to give a concert.
    C a solo violinist going to play in a concert in London.
    D an American musical agent who had an appointment with Sir Adrian Boult.

Second passage

TBA INDUSTRIAL Products produces asbestos textiles for brake linings. The company is just instituting a programme to reduce the asbestos in the air at the plant to a maximum 0.5 fibres per millilitre of air – the control limit imposed by the Health and Safety Executive responsible. With constant exposure to that level, according to a report by an Ontario Royal Commission, between one and four out of 100 people working for 25 years could expect to die of an asbestos-related cancer. Yet David Gee, health and safety officer of the General, Municipal and Boilermakers Union, accepts that the company should go no lower. Why?

Problem number one is assessing the risk and the difference that proposed safety measures would make to it. There are three basic categories, to which the HSE's policy-makers work – in the jargon, corpses, cancers and catastrophes.

"Corpses" are the victims of one-off accidents. A wealth of evidence on such accidents exists, and the effects of measures to combat them are easily calculated.

"Cancers", the killer diseases that can arise from working long periods in unsafe environments, are harder to assess. The diseases may not appear until years after the process was first initiated, and the relationship between cause and effect is often controversial.

Assessing the potential for "catastrophes" – like Bhopal, Seveso or Flixborough – in which tens of thousands of people can be affected is harder still. Such events are exceedingly rare so they cannot be predicted on the basis of past experience. Instead engineering experts think of everything that could go wrong – and of the things that could go wrong with the precautions. The probability of an accident is then expressed in terms of the number of likely catastrophes per 10,000 years, usually a fraction of one. This process yields an estimate of the risk of loss of life for each plant or process. The next stage is to put a money value on it.

The classic economist's calculation uses what is called the "human capital" approach. The dead person is valued as a machine who would otherwise have produced goods.

This callous calculus made no allowance for what most people would regard as the main cost of a lost life – the pain, grief and suffering. That has now changed, thanks to work by Professor Michael Jones-Lee and colleagues at Newcastle University. They asked members of the public what risks they would be prepared to run for what overall rewards. This process yields estimates of the subjective value of lives. The answer seems to come out between £1m and £2m.

31 Why is the company TBA Industrial Products about to reduce asbestos levels in the air at their plant?
   A To comply with a report by the Ontario Royal Commission.
   B Because the Union is demanding stricter safety measures.
   C Because present levels are above those set by the HSE.
   D To improve the quality of their brake linings.

32 "Cancers" are harder to assess than "corpses" because
   A the safety measures employed vary a great deal.
   B there are far more of them.
   C the wealth of evidence has not yet been analysed.
   D it is difficult to trace the cause of some diseases.

33 What does the assessment of the potential for "catastrophes" rely on?
   A An analysis of a few past disasters.
   B Mathematical probability calculations.
   C A comparison with 'cancers' and 'corpses'.
   D Reports of a company's capital.

34 The writer suggests that the "human capital" approach is
   A unreliable and risky.
   B invaluable.
   C too rough and ready.
   D clinical and inhumane.

35 A typical question posed to the public by Professor Jones-Lee and his colleagues would have been:
   A How much do you think a person's life is worth?
   B Would you say you enjoy taking risks at work?
   C How much would you work in an asbestos factory for?
   D What reward would you expect for saving someone's life?

Third passage

Extract 1

We, the undersigned, write with reference to the Hightown Local Plan, Consultative Draft, March 1985, published by the Hightown District Council.

While we understand the need for a Relief Road to ease the problems of increasing traffic in the area as a whole, we would like to express our concern at the proposed route. As shown in the Consultative Draft, the Relief Road will cross Fernwood Road, Golfcourse Way and High Lane, effectively cutting in half a prime residential area.

As residents of this particular area, we feel obliged to protest at the proposal on the following grounds:
- There will be a substantial increase in traffic in the area, not only with the through-traffic, but also from traffic joining the Relief Road at the junction planned close to Fernwood Road.
- At present, the area in question is a quiet residential area. With the Relief Road and the volume of traffic envisaged, there is no doubt that . . .

Extract 2

It is foreseen that the Relief Road will be a dual, two-lane carriageway and that there will be junctions at Fernwood Road and at the south end of High Lane. It is felt that such a road is required to allow for the growth of traffic envisaged over the next twenty years and that this route will be essential for through-traffic joining the Hightown Bypass. Thus the Relief Road and the Hightown Bypass together will provide substantial relief to the traffic problems experienced in recent years in the centre of Fernwood following the construction of the new Container Port at Highport in 1980.

It is intended that construction of the Relief Road be begun in 1989. This, however, will be subject to approval by regional and central government. The Planning Committee feel that the road is vital to a proper development of the area as a whole and that therefore delays should be avoided. Thus arrangements will be made, through public meetings, for direct representations to be made to the Council regarding the proposals.

Extract 3

Both John and I hope that you are all settling down OK. You must write and tell us what the new house is like.

By the way, your move was probably a good thing for you. We've just heard about the new Local Plan for Hightown and have been busy drumming up support to fight a proposal to bring a Relief Road right through here. In fact, as far as we can see, it would have run right along the back of your garden in Golfcourse Way. I can just imagine what Mike would have had to say about the prospect of massive lorries trundling past his back garden night and day! Fortunately, as far as the plans are concerned, we're not directly affected – I mean, the road won't go past our house – but it will cut through two or three roads here, which will mean that we'd obviously get a lot more traffic through this . . .

36 Which is the most likely end to the final sentence in Extract 1? '... there is no doubt that ...'
    A shopkeepers would flourish.
    B the district will suffer.
    C other roads will be needed.
    D it will become attractive to new residents.

37 Extract 2 is probably from
    A an official planning document.
    B an application by a firm of contractors.
    C a popular newspaper article.
    D a letter to a casual acquaintance.

38 The language of Extract 2 might best be described as
    A aggressive and hard-hitting.
    B impersonal and matter-of-fact.
    C tentative and vague.
    D friendly and persuasive.

39 It is possible that the writer of Extract 3
    A has just moved house.
    B also wrote Extract 2.
    C lives in Golfcourse Way.
    D also wrote Extract 1.

40 Which Extract refers to a cause of present traffic problems?
    A Extract 1.
    B Extract 2.
    C Extract 3.
    D None of them.

PAPER 2: COMPOSITION

Time: 2 hours

Write **two only** *of the following composition exercises. Your answers must follow exactly the instructions given. Write in pen, not pencil. You are allowed to make alterations, but see that your work is clear and easy to read.*

1. 'Our country's heritage must be preserved to pass on to our children.' Discuss. You may write in the form of a dialogue between two speakers, or in essay form. (About 350 words)

2. Write a description of the place (village, town, city, country, island, etc.) you would most like to live in. (About 350 words)

3. Imagine you are a magistrate in a court of law. Write a descriptive account of a busy working day. (About 350 words)

4. An English-language magazine to which you subscribe is appealing for short articles for a series that it hopes to run under the title *English Across the World*. Here is a brief extract from the Editor's appeal:

> What we are looking for are articles of about 350 words by learners from all parts of the world. We hope they will tell readers how long they have been learning the language, what kinds of materials they used and what methods their teachers employed; what they enjoyed while learning the language – and what they didn't enjoy; how much opportunity they had during their years of learning the language actually to use it, and so on. Articles which will give some indication to teachers and materials writers as to what learners really want and what they really enjoy will be particularly welcome.

Write an article to send in to the magazine. (And don't forget to give it a title or headline.)

5. *(This will be a choice of questions on the prescribed texts.)*

PAPER 3: USE OF ENGLISH

Time: 2 hours

Section A

1 *Fill each of the numbered blanks in the following passage with* **one** *suitable word.*

In . . . . (1) of the efforts of the media in recent years to disillusion us, the general picture . . . . (2) the ordinary public has of the 'author' is of . . . . (3) sitting hunched . . . . (4) a typewriter in solitude in a garret or some other place away from prying eyes. And not . . . . (5) that, but 'royalties', that name given historically to the financial rewards of the writing profession, ... (6) seem to be more than just 'wages' or 'a salary'. And . . . . (7) that's just . . . . (8) royalties are: they are certainly not the 'bonus' that my children always imagined them to . . . . (9) when they arrived from a publisher. My fault . . . . (10) not educating them properly, I suppose, but the receipt of a royalty cheque . . . . (11) always bring with it appeals from the children for extras, ... (12) they thought of . . . . (13) something akin . . . . (14) Christmas or birthday presents: it certainly wasn't money that . . . . (15) to be apportioned in the same way . . . . (16) others apportion their wages or salary. Indeed, ... (17) I not learned very early on in my writing career to see royalties as my 'salary' and apportion . . . . (18) carefully – much more carefully than other people, ... (19) they are an irregular form of income – I would long . . . . (20) have been in dire financial straits!

2 *Finish each of the following sentences in such a way that it means exactly the same as the sentence printed before it.*

Example: 'Remember to lock the door when you go out,' she said to him.
Answer: She reminded *him to lock the door when he went out.*

  a) I'm having a lot of trouble now because I lost my passport last week.
      If I ....

  b) When the police caught him, he was climbing over the garden wall.
      The police caught ....

  c) It's sad, but unemployment is unlikely to go down this year.
      Sad ....

  d) It is believed that the man escaped in a stolen car.
      The man is ....

  e) Since we had nothing else to do, we decided to go for a walk.
      Having ....

  f) 'Nothing will persuade me to sleep in that haunted house,' she said.
      She flatly ....

g) It wasn't necessary for them to call for help after all.
They ....

h) You won't find a more dedicated worker anywhere than Mrs Jones.
Nowhere ....

3 *Fill each of the blanks with a suitable word or phrase.*
Example: I went to the optician's last week *to have my eyes* tested.

a) What have you been doing? You .... that job ages ago!

b) Only after I had read the figures a few times .... what an awful mess the company was in.

c) So .... the meeting that it was hardly worth hiring such a large hall.

d) Members .... for the conference in April must do so by January 31st at the latest.

e) If you want to get his support, you'd .... antagonise him by mentioning the last project he was involved in.

f) 'Didn't you have a meal last night?'
'No. By the time I got home, the family .... !'

4 *For each of the sentences below, write a new sentence as similar as possible in meaning to the original sentence, but using the words given: these words* **must not be altered** *in any way.*

Example: The design on these hand-painted vases may vary slightly.
variation
Answer: There may be some slight variation in the design on these hand-painted vases.

a) I want to be left alone.
disturbed
....

b) He took the company to court on the grounds of unfair dismissal.
unfairly
....

c) We're likely to be a little late, I'm afraid.
every
....

d) The Committee said they liked the first proposal best.
preference
....

e) I really must answer all these letters.
get down
....

f) It's not your fault.
   blame
   ....

g) People seem to be criticising the police quite a lot nowadays.
   criticism
   ....

h) In a nutshell, the man's an idiot!
   bluntly
   ....

Section B

5 Read the passage opposite, then answer the questions below.

a) Why had the peregrine falcon flown against the oil executive's window?

b) What did the peregrine's accident (described in paragraphs 1 and 2) have to do with Californian ornithologists?

c) Why are peregrine falcons in California in danger of extinction?

d) What effect do you think the writer tries to create with the expression 'upon which the peregrine dines' (lines 36–37)?

e) Explain in your own words the phrase 'scrapes together' (line 45).

f) Why did ornithologists think the peregrines would have a better chance of survival in the city?

g) How did the bird which flew against the oil executive's window survive?

h) Apart from skyscrapers, what other danger(s) do the birds have to avoid?

i) Explain the sentence 'They make wily urban hunters' (lines 74–75).

j) Why were ornithologists both pleased *and* worried last March?

k) How have city pigeons learned to escape attacks from peregrines?

l) Explain the phrase 'littered with scraps' (line 111).

m) Why, according to the writer, were the peregrines still taking in DDT?

n) How did the peregrines react to being given substitute young?

o) In one paragraph of 50–100 words, summarise the experiment being carried out in Los Angeles to save the peregrine falcon, and give a brief indication of its success or failure.

Eyrie of the city falcon

THE OIL executive was working his desk computer on the 30th floor of Los Angeles' Arco Tower. The last thing he expected was a knock on the window.

He whirled around in his chair to see an angry peregrine falcon bounce off the window in a bluish-grey spray of feathers and tumble through the wintery smog towards the plaza nearly 500 ft below. The bird of prey had seen its own reflection in the mirrored skyscraper, mistaken it for a rival and attacked.

As the peregrine – described as the world's most successful flying bird – plummeted towards a congregation of unsuspecting office workers far below, the hopes of American birdwatchers fell with him. For this falcon was part of an odd experiment to save the breed from extinction by adapting it to big city life.

In California, most of the small birds upon which the peregrine dines are contaminated with DDT. When the female peregrine lays eggs, the toxic chemicals have usually made the shell so thin that they crack on the gravel nests that the falcon scrapes together on cliff edges. So ornithologists decided that maybe a diet of city pigeons fattened on discarded McDonald's hamburgers was more wholesome for the peregrines than a dose of DDT.

Like the hero in a two-reeler, the battered bird regained consciousness seconds before crashing and flapped back up to its nesting mate on the ledge of the Union Bank building. In fact, this pair of falcons and two others living on different spires around greater Los Angeles are surviving better in the city than many of its human inhabitants.

Downtown LA swarms with helicopters but the peregrines have learned to steer clear of them as they would, say, of an eagle in the wild. They make wily urban hunters. A favourite tactic is to descend from a skyscraper in a tight, skimming spiral, accelerating to more than 150 mph, and ambush the prey from the rear, punching the bird senseless with its talons bunched into a fist.

The peregrine falcon

Last March, observers from the Peregrine Fund, which sponsors the project along with the Western Foundation of Vertebrate Zoology, looked through their binoculars and saw four scarlet eggs the size of apples sitting in the nest. But the inexperienced parents smashed one egg on the ledge below. Another egg cracked because its shell was so thin. Ornithologists blame this on DDT.

That is because a peregrine falcon will only eat birds it grabs in spectacular mid-air dives. So once the birds realised a hawk was in their territory, they began to flutter no higher than the tables in the outdoor restaurants, which are littered with scraps. Paul Young, who keeps watch on the peregrines from his perch in the Arco law library, says the pigeons can recognise the hawk's high-speed silhouette. So migratory birds – poisoned with DDT – were all that the peregrines could snatch.

Ornithologists stole the two remaining eggs, and several weeks later, replaced them with fledgling peregrines. Instead of tossing these helpless strangers over the ledge, the adults reacted with the proper parental instincts. The survival of future generations of city falcons depends on how quickly they can learn to corner their intended prey, the streetwise pigeon.

Tim McGirk

PAPER 4: LISTENING COMPREHENSION
Time: approx. 30 minutes

First part

For questions 1–7 tick (√) whether the statements are true or false, according to what you hear.

		True	False	
1	The guest speaker was one of the school's first pupils.			1
2	Not all its pupils have been a credit to the school.			2
3	The school has always been co-educational.			3
4	The guest speaker has written at least four plays.			4
5	His most recent hit is a comedy.			5
6	His first novel won a literary prize.			6
7	The Headmaster once criticised the guest's English.			7

Second part

Read this small newspaper advertisement and then, as you listen, write corrections in the right-hand column for questions 8–13, according to what you hear.

HURRY! HURRY! HURRY!
**WORLDWIDE TRAVEL is offering 12 places on a 14-day holiday to Spain! Full-board for only £210. Ideal for couples. Available March and April. First-class hotel accommodation.
Ring Worldwide Travel: 429807**

Write your corrections to the advertisement here:

8 ....
9 ....
10 ....
11 ....
12 ....
13 ....

Third part

For each of the questions 14–18, put a tick (√) in one of the boxes, A, B, C or D, according to what you hear.

14 Although the incident in Mad Mike's café was a serious one,
   A it was soon ended by an alert police force.
   B it had some good moments.
   C it only came to light some time after the event.
   D it was an isolated occurrence in an otherwise peaceful night.

15 As far as Mr Watson was concerned, last night's trouble
   A was the first in nearly twenty years.
   B was worse than anything he had experienced before.
   C unfortunately started outside his café.
   D was the first outbreak of violence this year.

16 It would seem that the Broadmoor fans were
   A looking for trouble.
   B not to blame for what happened.
   C wearing clearly identifiable clothes.
   D frequent visitors to the café.

17 What opinion does the Police Superintendent express?
   A The incident had little to do with the police.
   B The match was probably over-supervised by the police.
   C He may have been guilty of lack of foresight.
   D The courts must give offenders more severe punishments.

18 What will be one effect of the incident?
   A It will disappoint politicians responsible for fans' conduct.
   B It will provide government with much-needed ammunition.
   C It will do much to reduce criticism of police tactics.
   D It will lead to a top-level meeting soon.

Fourth part

For each of the questions 19–24, put a tick (√) in one of the boxes, A, B, C or D, according to what you hear.

19 What does the writer tell us about his meeting with the woman?
   A It was arranged long before.
   B It was to do with a recent conference.
   C It had been fixed the night before.
   D It was a chance occurrence.

20 When they had finished lunch,
   A the woman insisted on paying for them both.
   B they had to walk down the muddy hotel footpath.
   C the man found very little to talk about.
   D they walked by the river and reminisced.

21 What do we learn about the woman's English?
   A It improved during the afternoon.
   B It had not improved since their last meeting.
   C It was still excellent.
   D It had improved since they last met.

22 When the woman invited the writer home with her,
   A he already knew her mother had died.
   B he had already started saying goodbye.
   C they were drinking cognac near the square.
   D it was already evening.

23 What did the writer find unusual about the little girl?
   A She spoke Chinese.
   B She came in unnoticed.
   C She looked innocent.
   D She spoke in an unemotional way.

24 Although he had once known the woman very well, the writer
   A spoke only a little Chinese.
   B had never met her mother.
   C failed to recognise the little girl.
   D had forgotten a lot about her.

Exam One

PAPER 5: INTERVIEW

Time: approx. 15 minutes

1. *Study this photo carefully, then describe it and be prepared to discuss one or more of the related topics (Note: In the Cambridge Proficiency Exam Interview, you will only see the photo; you will **not** see any instructions or discussion topics.)*

Describe:	*Discuss one of these:*
– the people (and the attitude of the woman towards the men).	– strikes and picketing.
– the scene.	– different jobs/professions and their value.
	– protests and demonstrations.

2. *Study one of the two passages for a few moments. Then say **a)** where you think it might have come from, and **b)** who might have said or written it (to whom and when). Finally, what is your reaction to the passage?*

i) | In a report out today, the Government is criticised for not taking early action to counteract growing unemployment. According to NIC, the National Industrial Council, the Government has constantly discounted fears that the steady growth in unemployment will contribute significantly to a decline in the production industry.

ii) When I got my redundancy notice, I didn't believe it. I just didn't believe it. I knew the firm was laying people off, but I didn't think I'd be one of them. After all, I'd been there for something like 25 years, and I'd only just been promoted to run a new Apprentice Training Scheme they were planning to start up. Oh, I got quite good redundancy money, but it'll be very difficult for me to get another job.

3 *This table shows the pay rises that different groups of workers in the UK have received during the past year. Study it carefully, then be prepared to discuss the topics and questions below.*

IMPORTANT PAY DEALS SO FAR

Group	Numbers	Settlement (%)	Comment
Local authority manual workers	1 million	6.7–12	Job evaluation to follow
Engineering	1 million	5.5	Minimum rates only
Vauxhall (cars)	15,000	13	2-year deal
National Coal Board	30,000	6–7	Related to productivity
Govt. engineers and technologists	40,000	13.3–26.1	Over three years on top of annual award
Mirror Group Newspapers	6,000	10	2-stage offer linked to 2,000 redundances
Esso tanker drivers	1,700	9	Flexibility deal on top
Ford (cars)	37,500	3–5	2 years offer, up to 10% more available for efficiency measures
Fire service	43,000	7.2	Index-linked to average earnings
Safeway (supermarkets)	1,000	8.7–15.8	

Which group of workers have had the largest pay rises? Why, do you think?
What might be the effect on the public of certain pay rises? (Cost of goods, services, etc.)
How do such pay rises compare with those in your country?

and/or

4 *Work in pairs. While you read this, your partner will read another report on page 53. Read this newspaper report and then tell your partner about it in your own words. Tell him or her what you think about the implications of the report and ask for his or her comments.*

Train driver attacked

A Southern Region train driver who refused to go on strike was admitted to hospital last night suffering from cuts and bruises to his head and back.

Mr Tom Gould (49) was walking to work in defiance of a union call to strike when he was attacked by four men. According to Mr Gould, the men approached him and tried to persuade him not to go to work, but to return home. When he told them he was determined to go on the night shift, they beat him around the head and back.

Mr Gould stated: 'I refuse to be intimidated by such tactics. I don't agree with the strike and I shall be going to work again tomorrow night.'

When asked about the incident, the local union spokesman declined to comment.

Exam Two

PAPER 1: READING COMPREHENSION

Time: 1 hour

This Paper is in two parts, Section A and Section B. For each question you answer correctly in Section A you gain one mark; for each question you answer correctly in Section B you gain two marks. No marks are deducted for wrong answers. Answer all the questions. Indicate your choice of answer in every case on a separate sheet. Follow carefully the instructions about how to record your answers.

Section A

In this Section you must choose the word or phrase which best completes each sentence. For each question, 1 to 25, indicate on your answer sheet the letter A, B, C or D against the number of the question.

1 The thought of taking such an examination had never for one moment . . . . my head.
   A entered   B occurred   C crossed   D slipped

2 The chances of a repetition of these events are . . . . indeed.
   A distant   B slim   C unlikely   D narrow

3 She . . . . out of the house as fast as her legs would carry her.
   A strolled   B dashed   C ambled   D plunged

4 Certain details in the contract still remain to be . . . . out.
   A flattened   B dealt   C ironed   D borne

5 . . . . little we may like it, old age comes to most of us.
   A Despite   B However   C So   D As

6 'But son,' I told him, 'you're my own . . . .'
   A heart to heart   B body and soul   C flesh and blood   D skin and bone

7 For a while I was at a . . . . to know what to say.
   A blank   B pain   C loss   D crisis

8 The easiest way to get this nut off the bolt would be to use a . . . .
   A spanner   B winch   C screwdriver   D jack

9 After the extravagant claims of the advance publicity, the film was a great . . . .
   A buildup   B letdown   C breakout   D fallout

10 Which . . . . do you propose to play this piece in?
   A notes   B key   C chord   D score

11 We are totally opposed . . . . any changes being made in the proposals as they stand.
   A of   B against   C towards   D to

12 During Queen Elizabeth's ...., Britain's role in the world has changed dramatically.
   A ruling   B monarchy   C reign   D coronation

13 A golden handshake may have a .... effect when one is dealt the blow of redundancy.
   A cushioning   B pillowing   C carpeting   D curtaining

14 The baby at the centre of the controversy has been made a .... of court.
   A progeny   B child   C protégé   D ward

15 The late Rev. Ivor Jones will be .... missed.
   A sadly   B unhappily   C regrettably   D deeply

16 The removal of magazines from this room is strictly ....
   A discouraged   B forbidden   C deterred   D illicit

17 The government may be forced to .... their privatisation plans for the time being.
   A shelve   B implement   C go ahead with   D cancel

18 His comments .... little or no relation to the facts and figures of the case.
   A reflect   B give   C bear   D possess

19 I was awakened early in the morning by the .... of sheep in the fields outside my window.
   A baying   B braying   C neighing   D bleating

20 I must confess I was .... myself with rage.
   A above   B outside   C beside   D beyond

21 To all intents and ...., the estimates are identical.
   A meanings   B dealings   C concepts   D purposes

22 'The 20-year policy would be a good investment,' said the insurance agent, '........ you wanted to cash it in within the first ten years.'
   A even though   B in case   C even if   D lest

23 I have a .... headache.
   A spitting   B raving   C splitting   D burning

24 The imposition of martial law has been accompanied by an after-dark ....
   A remand   B curfew   C recession   D custody

25 You .... us to believe that service and V.A.T. would be included.
   A tricked   B let   C made   D led

Section B

In this Section you will find after each of the passages a number of questions or unfinished statements about the passage, each with four suggested answers or ways of finishing. You must choose the one which you think fits best. For each question, 26 to 40, **indicate on your answer sheet** *the letter A, B, C or D against the number of the question. Give* **one answer only** *to each question. Read each passage right through before choosing your answers.*

First passage

I got used, too, to my employer's violent changes of front. There was one morning when Siegfried came down to breakfast, rubbing a hand wearily over red-rimmed eyes.

'Out at 4 a.m.,' he groaned, buttering his toast listlessly. 'And I don't like to have to say this, James, but it's all your fault.'

'My fault?' I said, startled.

'Yes, lad, your fault. This was a cow with a mild impaction of the rumen. The farmer had been mucking about with it himself for days; a pint of linseed oil one day, a bit of bicarb and ginger the next, and at four o'clock in the morning he decides it is time to call the vet. When I pointed out it could have waited a few hours more he said Mr Herriot told him never to hesitate to ring – he'd come out any hour of the day or night.'

He tapped the top of his egg as though the effort was almost too much for him. 'Well, it's all very well being conscientious and all that, but if a thing has waited several days it can wait till morning. You're spoiling these chaps, James, and I'm getting the backwash of it. I'm sick and tired of being dragged out of bed for trifles.'

'I'm truly sorry, Siegfried. I honestly had no wish to do that to you. Maybe it's just my inexperience. If I didn't go out, I'd be worried the animal might die. If I left it till morning and it died, how would I feel?'

'That's all right,' snapped Siegfried. 'There's nothing like a dead animal to bring them to their senses. They'll call us out a bit earlier next time.'

I absorbed this bit of advice and tried to act on it. A week later, Siegfried said he wanted a word with me.

'James, I know you won't mind my saying this, but old Sumner was complaining to me today. He says he rang you the other night and you refused to come out to his cow. He's a good client, you know, and a very nice fellow, but he was quite shirty about it. We don't want to lose a chap like that.'

'But it was just a chronic mastitis,' I said. 'A bit of thickening in the milk, that's all. He'd been dosing it himself for nearly a week with some quack remedy. The cow was eating all right, so I thought it would be quite safe to leave it till next day.'

Siegfried put a hand on my shoulder and an excessively patient look spread over his face. I steeled myself. I didn't mind his impatience; I was used to it and could stand it. But the patience was hard to take.

'James,' he said in a gentle voice, 'there is one fundamental rule in our job which transcends all others, and I'll tell you what it is. YOU MUST ATTEND. That is it and it ought to be written on your soul in letters of fire.'

26 Siegfried was not at his best on the first morning because
   A his breakfast was not to his liking.
   B he had been called out during the night.
   C he had been woken up early for breakfast.
   D the farmer hadn't tried to cure the cow himself.

27 James was criticised that morning for being too
   A well-meaning.
   B callous.
   C careless.
   D inexperienced.

28 James thought it was all right to leave Sumner's cow till next day because
    A that was what Siegfried had advised.
    B Sumner had said there was no urgency.
    C he knew he could do nothing to save the animal.
    D Sumner never paid his bills on time.

29 The impression James gives of Siegfried is that of
    A a fairly easy-going, generous employer.
    B someone rather pompous and unpredictable.
    C a conscientious but senile old man.
    D an insufferable, tyrannical boss.

30 'You must attend', in the context of the passage, means:
    A You must follow your conscience.
    B You must use your powers of discretion.
    C You must go out whenever you are called.
    D You must pay close attention at all times.

Second passage

In the immediate post-war years, the city of Birmingham scheduled some 50,000 small working class cottages as slums due for demolition. Today that process is nearly complete. Yet it is clear that, quite apart from any question of race, an environmental problem remains. The expectation built into the planning policies of 1945 was that in the foreseeable future the city would be a better place to live in. But now that slum clearance has run its course, there seems to be universal agreement that the total environment where the slums once stood is more depressing than ever.

For the past ten years the slum clearance areas have looked like bomb sites. The buildings and places which survive do so on islands in a sea of rubble and ash. When the slums were there they supported an organic community life and each building, each activity, fitted in as part of the whole. But now that they have been destroyed, nothing meaningful appears to remain, or rather those activities which do go on do not seem to have any meaningful relation to the place. They happen there because it is an empty stage which no-one is using any more.

Typical of the inner-city in this sense is the Birmingham City Football Ground. Standing in unsplendid isolation on what is now wasteland on the edge of Small Heath, it brings into the area a stage army on twenty or so Saturdays a year who come and cheer and then go away again with little concern any more for the place where they have done their cheering. Even they, however, have revolted recently. 'The ground' says the leader of the revolt, 'is a slum', thus putting his finger on the fact that the demolition of houses creates rather than solves problems of the inner-city.

A new element has now come upon the scene in the inner-city in the form of the tower block. Somehow it doesn't seem to be what Le Corbusier and the planners who wrote those post-war Pelicans intended. The public spaces either haven't yet been developed or are more meanly conceived, and the corridors and lifts are places of horror. In fact these places were always suspect. They had no legitimacy in the minds of the public as suburban family housing had, and those who were placed there felt that they had been cheated. Along with the decaying elements, therefore, that which had been conceived as part of the brave new world was part of the problem.

31 The past few decades in Birmingham have proved that slum clearance
    A will usually take longer than expected.
    B creates as many problems as it solves.
    C often raises racial issues.
    D always achieves its aims, if well planned.

32 According to the passage, now that the slum dwellings have gone,
    A no one does anything at all in those areas.
    B urban theatrical life has gone, too.
    C rebuilding can start almost immediately.
    D the area is extremely unattractive.

33 According to the author, a number of Birmingham City football fans
    A seem to be reluctant to continue supporting their team.
    B are as rebellious as any other club's supporters.
    C get necessary release from watching their team play.
    D are concerned about the future of that part of Birmingham.

34 What did people think about tower blocks when they were first built?
    A Town planners thought they were badly conceived.
    B The public compared them with rural housing.
    C The man in the street mistrusted them.
    D People thought them an improvement on suburban housing.

35 From the style in which it's written, this passage was almost certainly taken from
    A an official local planning report.
    B a novel set in Birmingham.
    C a history of the Industrial Revolution.
    D a sociology textbook.

Third passage

A
Chiropodist

If you can tolerate smelly feet, the public belief that you are only a corn cutter and, to quote one chiropodist, "the blue-rinsed matrons who believe that they can get away with putting size eight feet into size five winklepickers", this is one of the more attractive para-medical careers. There is a nationwide shortage of qualified people: a high professional retirement rate in the near future, growing public consciousness of footcare, and the national craze for jogging are likely to increase opportunities over the next decade. Chiropodists treat feet, prescribe the necessary appliances and sometimes make them, though anything but the most minor surgery must be performed by a doctor.

B
Occupational Therapist

"I can't sew, knit, draw or make cuddly toys," said one occupational therapist desperately. The profession still suffers from its historical associations with basketwork in bleak rooms in hospital annexes. Modern therapy is far more sophisticated; its general brief is to help people who are handicapped or recovering from serious mental or physical illness (including alcoholism or drug dependence) to adapt to normal life. As well as devising courses to exercise body and mind, occupational therapists teach people how to live in wheelchairs or to work with one arm. They are more concerned with operating washing machines, cookers and lathes than with knitting needles.

C
Veterinary Surgeon

Veterinary science is one of the most competitive subjects for university entry – a few years ago, there were five applicants for each of the 335 annual places. But the work to get there is nothing to what's involved in the five or six-year course itself. Many students are shocked by the sheer volume of facts. Remember that, while doctors specialise in particular branches of human medicine, vets must cover all aspects of a huge variety of living organisms. That is the attraction, as well as the difficulty of the job. "I can be diagnostician, physician, surgeon, radiographer and all, following the case through from start to finish," said one vet.

D
Dietitian

Dietetics is a rising profession, which has become more authoritative, vocal and self-confident over the past decade. Not so long ago, doctors tended to regard dietitians as fussy busy-bodies who should be kept out of harm's way in the hospital kitchens. Nowadays, they are treated with increasing deference, particularly since high-fibre diets started reducing hospital bills for constipation drugs. The public still assumes that their main job is advising people how to lose weight. But this is only a very small part of their work.

36 Which of the professions seems to be many jobs in one?
   A   B   C   D

37 Which profession would be chosen by a student desperate not to be unemployed?
   A   B   C   D

38 Which profession would appear to be most difficult to break into?
   A   B   C   D

39 Which profession is enjoying a status and esteem not known before?
   A   B   C   D

40 Three of the four extracts suggest that the public underrates the profession. Which one (of the four) doesn't suggest that?
   A   B   C   D

PAPER 2: COMPOSITION

Time: 2 hours

*Write **two only** of the following composition exercises. Your answers must follow exactly the instructions given. Write in pen, not pencil. You are allowed to make alterations, but see that your work is clear and easy to read.*

1 Discuss the opinion that 'television not only reports news, but also influences the news'. (About 350 words)

2 Suggest some ways in which education might be improved in your country. (About 350 words)

3 Write a short story which ends as follows: '. . . So that's how I finally succeeded in overcoming my fear of spiders.' (About 350 words)

4 You are looking for a job in your summer holidays and recently saw this advertisement in an English newspaper in your country. Write a letter of application. (About 300 words)

> **Courier Wanted**
> Recognised English language school on south coast of England requires, for July and August, a courier to accompany groups of students (ages 12–17) travelling to and from courses at the school. The successful applicant must have a good command of English and must speak at least two other European languages fluently. He or she must also have had experience in dealing with youngsters (teaching, youth training work, etc.) and be conversant with all kinds of travel and travel arrangements. Please apply in writing, giving brief curriculum vitae and qualifications. Full application form and details re remuneration and conditions will be sent by return.

5 *(This will be a choice of questions on the prescribed texts.)*

PAPER 3: USE OF ENGLISH

Time: 2 hours

Section A

1 *Fill each of the numbered blanks in the following passage with* **one** *suitable word.*

It has been written so often that it .... (1) bears repeating, but there is .... (2) new in this world. The campaign for animal rights .... (3) to be gaining prominence in the 1980s, but one man in Britain was fighting for just such rights well .... (4) 150 years ago.

Richard Martin, who earned the nickname of 'Humanity Dick', was born in Dublin in 1754 and died in Boulogne, France, in 1834. .... (5) his adult life he championed the rights of animals to humane treatment. .... (6) born in Ireland, he was sent to school at Harrow in England, ... (7) he was influenced by Dr Samuel Parr, a man who believed children .... (8) be taught to be kind to animals. Martin went to Cambridge and .... (9) on to Kings' Inns where he studied law. On .... (10) an M.P. at Westminster (after the Act of Union between Britain and Ireland in 1800), Martin supported a Bill to .... (11) bull-baiting abolished. The Bill was defeated, as .... (12) another to prevent malicious cruelty .... (13) horses, sheep and dogs a few years later, but Martin soldiered on. Finally, in 1822, an Act known .... (14) Martin's Act was passed .... (15) both Houses of Parliament which gave some protection to animals. Sadly, it was only in 1835, the year after his death, ... (16) a law was passed .... (17) the 1822 Act to include bulls and domestic animals, to improve conditions in slaughterhouses and effectively to .... (18) an end to bull-baiting and cock-fighting.

Perhaps Martin's finest achievement was his help in .... (19) setting-up of a Society for the Prevention of Cruelty to Animals, ... (20) aims were to educate the public and to see that the law of 1822 was implemented.

2 *Finish each of the following sentences in such a way that it means exactly the same as the sentence printed before it.*

Example: They'll do the job by Friday.
Answer: The job *will be done by Friday.*

a) She had hardly begun to speak before people started interrupting her.
Hardly ....

b) It was a bit difficult to get into work this morning.
Getting ....

c) We regret to inform you that your application has not been successful.
Much to ....

d) He knows nearly everything there is to know about whales.
There's ....

e) If we can solve the problem soon, it will be better for all concerned.
The sooner ....

f) The demand was so great that they had to reprint the book immediately.
So ....

g) I'm absolutely sure that they weren't playing in this weather.
They can't ....

h) 'I did not steal the car,' he said. 'I just *borrowed* it.'
He denied .... but admitted ....

3 Fill each of the blanks with a suitable word or phrase.

Example: <u>The longer</u> we stay here, the less time we'll have to look at the cathedral.

a) Look at the length of your hair! It's about time you ....

b) I wouldn't have hit the other car if I .... where I was going.

c) He works, or .... a year or so ago, for a computer company.

d) I object most strongly .... dirty jobs like that.

e) They were waving their arms about a lot, so they .... an argument, I suppose, but I couldn't see very well from so far away.

f) Little .... that we've organised a surprise party for her.

4 For each of the sentences below, write a new sentence as similar as possible in meaning to the original sentence, but using the words given: these words **must not be altered** in any way.

Example: She could hardly see.
virtually
Answer: She was virtually blind.

a) I'm dying to meet them.
wait
....

b) They lay on the beach the whole week sunbathing.
spent
....

c) I seriously doubt whether this will work.
doubts
....

d) He's always found it very difficult to learn English.
difficulty
....

e) I have no intention of giving up now.
intend
....

f) They've always been allowed to do what they want.
freedom
....

g) This is quite a common occurrence.
frequently
....

h) Something told me to say exactly what I thought, but I didn't.
sorely
....

Section B

5   *Read the following passage, then answer the questions which follow it.*

Plato called them 'children of gold' who should be encouraged in the study of philosophy and metaphysics. In this age the budding of genius in the very young is not always an occasion for celebration.

There was a recent case of a mother who took her three-year-old daughter along on a visit to a clinic only to have her offspring entertain the waiting-room with a piping rendition of a medical pamphlet. Until that moment the mother didn't know her daughter could read. The child's 'gift' was an embarrassment.

Against that there are cases of genius spotted early and lovingly refined. Ruth Lawrence, aged 13, the mathematics prodigy now in her second year at Oxford University, is an illustration. Taught by her father since infancy, she never went to a normal school.

Yet both categories of prodigy – the coincidental and the coached — can experience problems that most children are lucky enough to avoid. In young Ruth's case the separation from children of her own age is the most obvious handicap. Studies have shown that accelerating a child's education by a year may be beneficial, but that larger leaps forward can often induce feelings of isolation. Ruth has vaulted six years.

The stabilising factor in her case is that mathematicians need to excel early and Ruth is scarcely ahead of schedule in her ambition to become Britain's youngest ever professor of mathematics.

Anita Straker, author of *Mathematics for Gifted Pupils*, thought that Ruth would have no motivation problems as an adolescent but that she, like all young mathematicians, should be prepared for the slackening of creative energy that almost invariably takes place by the late twenties. In general, she thought that prodigies in subjects like maths, computers and music were better appreciated by the adult world. Early geniuses in other subjects might not be so lucky.

One reason, particularly in the computer field, may be that the kids are often brighter than the grown-ups. Thus the school board in Montana recently hired Mike Hamaoka, aged 13, to teach teachers computer techniques. Another boy of the same age, Eugene Volokh, was taken on to the payroll of a California computer company at £300 a week.

Prodigies in music can look to the role models of Mozart and Menuhin and be persuaded that there is never a moment to lose however young they are. Literature, primarily the product of an adult consciousness, offers fewer models of this type, though Goethe and John Stuart Mill were reading Greek at the age of three. And Thomas Babington Macaulay, the great 19th century historian, was just over a year old when he posed his first question: 'Is the smoke of that chimney coming from hell?'

Precocity can however be perceived as a liability. David Lewis, a research psychologist and the author of *How To Be A Gifted Parent*, is struck by how often parents feel uneasy about giftedness in their children. 'There are exceptions of course, but they're not like pushy show-biz mums. They're often really troubled by their kid's apparent difference from others – sometimes with reason.'

a) The writer suggests that in this day and age we might not altogether agree with Plato's description of prodigies as 'children of gold'. Why?

b) Explain the phrase 'a piping rendition' (lines 5–6).

c) While both are examples of child prodigies, how are the three-year-old and the 13-year-old girls different?

d) How do we know that Ruth's genius was 'spotted early'?

e) What effect could being separated from children of her own age have on Ruth?

f) Why do you think the writer chose to use the word 'vaulted' (line 16)?

g) Why does the writer say that 'Ruth is scarcely ahead of schedule' (lines 17–18)?

h) According to Anita Straker, what happens to mathematicians in their late twenties?

i) Why is it suggested that it is easier for children to be prodigies in maths, computers and music than in many other subjects?

j) Mike Hamaoka and Eugene Volokh are quoted as examples of – what?

k) Explain the phrase 'taken on to the payroll' (line 29).

l) Why does the writer suggest there have been few prodigies in literature?

m) In what way might precocity (= an unusually early development of mind or body) be 'a liability' (line 36).

n) Explain in your own words the phrase 'pushy show-biz mums' (line 39).

o) Summarise in 50–100 words what the passage says about child prodigies.

PAPER 4: LISTENING COMPREHENSION

Time: approx. 30 minutes

First part

For each of the questions 1–5, put a tick (√) in one of the boxes A, B, C or D, according to what you hear.

1. An eponym is
   - A a word which describes any everyday article.
   - B a fascinating phrase which catches a reader's eye.
   - C an expression which a famous person has used.
   - D a word or phrase which comes from somebody's name.

2. 'Wellies' were originally
   - A 'Wellesley boots'.
   - B waterproof rubber boots.
   - C Iron Duke boots.
   - D made of leather.

3. Where did the word 'hooligan' come from?
   - A It was borrowed from a foreign language.
   - B It came from a book by Clarence Rook.
   - C A man called Partidge invented it.
   - D It was invented early this century to describe football fans.

4. The original 'nosey parker' was
   - A a sixteenth-century priest.
   - B someone who prayed too long and frequently.
   - C a bishop turned businessman.
   - D a fanatically career-minded person.

5. The derivation of 'blanket' is different from the others described in that
   - A the word originated in the 1450s.
   - B it was originally the name of a machine.
   - C it is the manufacturer's name.
   - D it was a kind of bed.

Second part

To answer questions 6–11, fill in the missing information on the hotel advance bookings sheet below.

Whitechapel Hotel			Advance Bookings		
Name(s) and Initials	Nationality	Contact Tel. No. (Area code first)	Type of room	Nights	Charge per night
Miss C.R. ROGERS	Canadian	none	Single with shower	24/4 –28/4	£25.00
Mr. and Mrs. J.T. SMYTHE	British	0202- 679335	Twin- bedded	26/4 —?	£27.50
6	7	8	9	10	11 ....

Third part

Study the list of places and look at the map below. To answer questions 12–18, write the number of the place (in each case) in the appropriate box on the map to indicate the location.
NOTE: The list of places is not in the same order as they appear on cassette.

12 casino
13 castle
14 cinema
15 coach station
16 art gallery
17 railway station
18 theatre

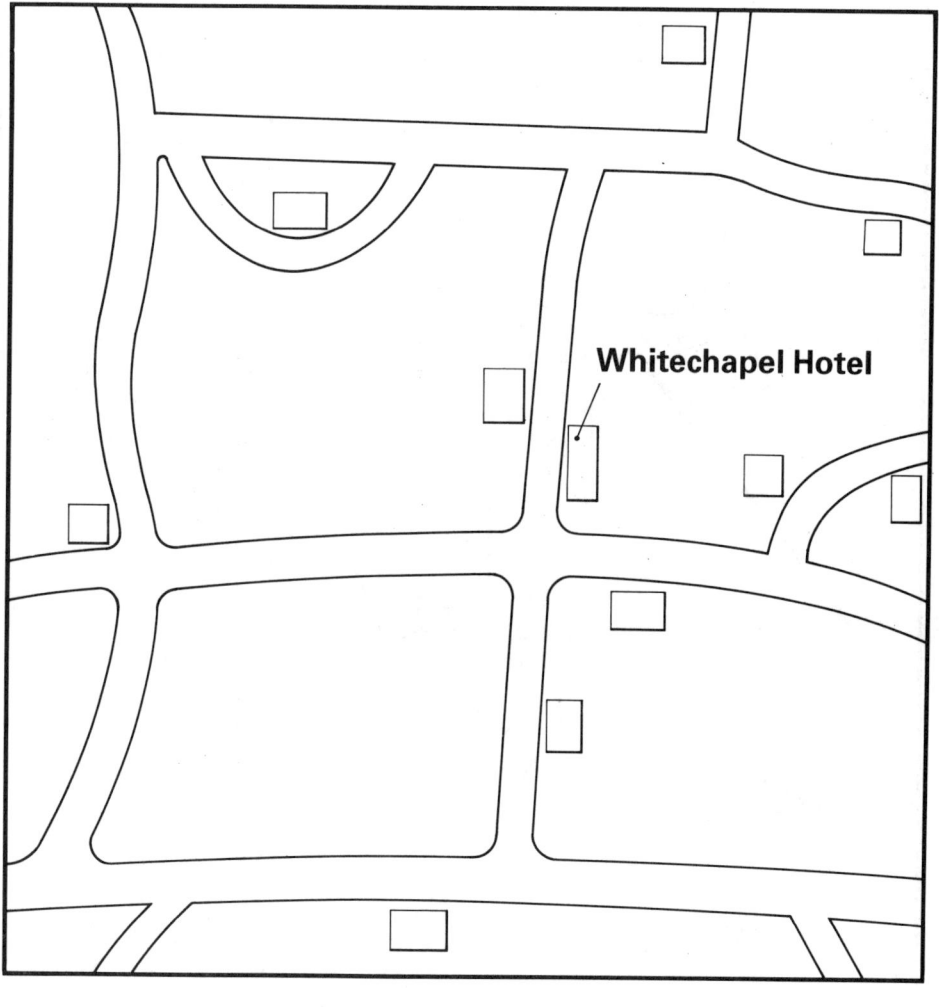

Fourth part

To answer questions 19–27, write the numbers 1 to 9 in the boxes beside the pictures below, according to the order in which they are to be used, and according to the 'instructor'.

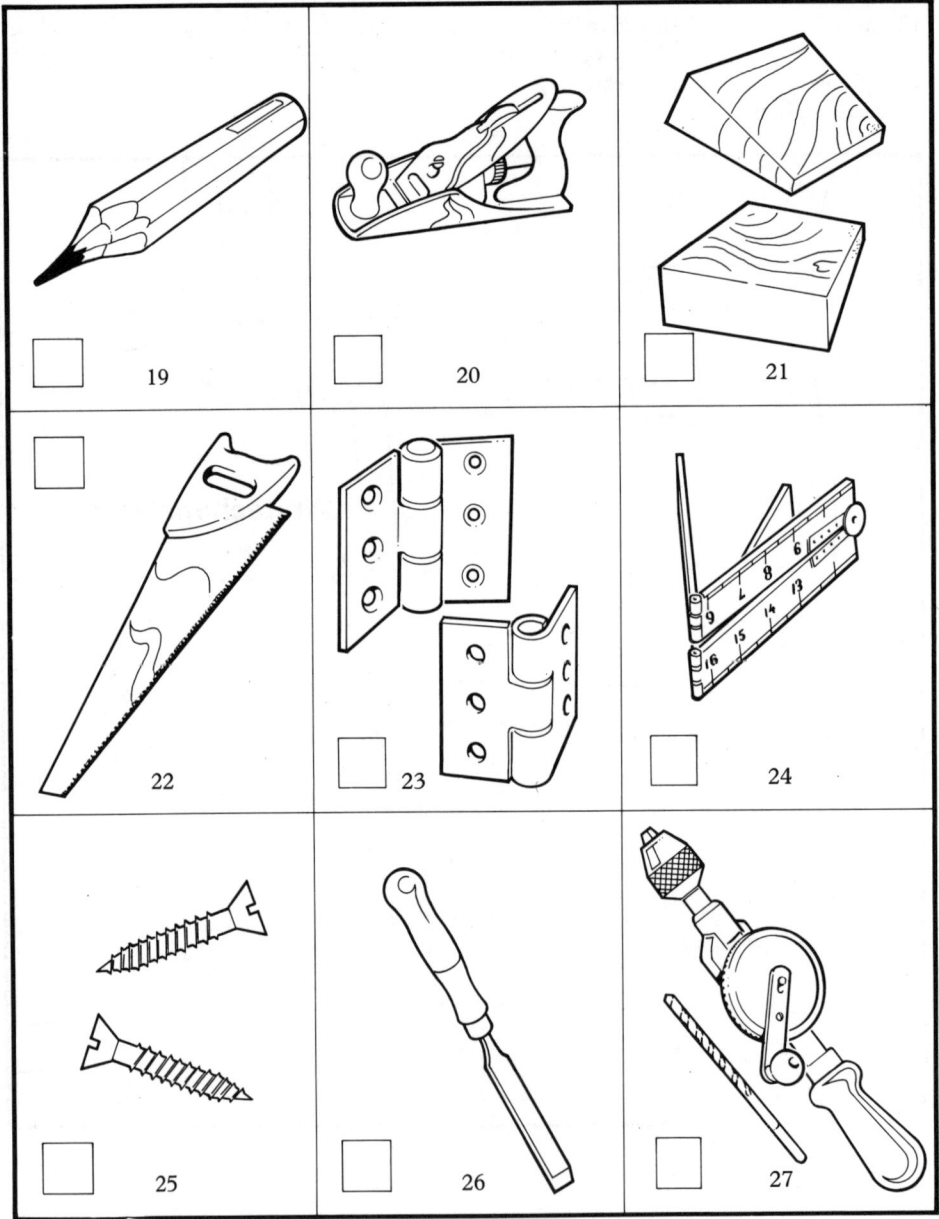

PAPER 5: INTERVIEW

Time: approx. 15 minutes

1 *Study this photo carefully, then describe it and be prepared to discuss one or more of the related topics (Note: In the Cambridge Proficiency Exam Interview, you will only see the photo; you will **not** see any instructions or discussion topics.)*

Describe:
− the people.
− their clothes and equipment.
− the scene.
− the activity.

Discuss one of these:
− climbing, mountaineering and other 'dangerous' sports.
− the attraction of different sports.
− the sports 'industry' (for equipment etc.)

2 *Study one of these passages for a few moments. Then say **a)** where you think it might have come from, and **b)** who might have said or written it (to whom and when). Finally, what is your reaction to the passage?*

i)	Lost for something to do evenings and weekends? Then why not come down to the Langfort Leisure Centre − and bring your friends or the family? The Centre's open seven days a week, 9 in the morning to 10 at night. It boasts an Olympic-size swimming-pool, a gymnasium, and squash and badminton courts − *and* a first-class self-service restaurant. Whatever the weather, come on in − the water's lovely! Remember: the Langfort Leisure Centre.
ii)	The ball may be moved with the stick only. A player must not pick up or throw the ball with her hands, or propel the ball forward in any way with her body. *A rising ball may, however, be caught, but it must be released immediately into play by dropping it to the ground.*

3 *This is from an 'Activity Holidays' brochure. Study it carefully and then be prepared to discuss the questions and topics below.*

Is there some sporting activity that you've longed to try...

...but never quite known how to go about organising it? If you have, now's your chance – because all you have to do is make your choice, book your weekend, and leave the rest to us. All prices include 2 nights' bed and breakfast.

PARACHUTING

It takes a special sort of nerve to parachute – but it's an exhilarating experience. Based at either Basingstoke or Leyland, you can take a 2-day training course at a British Parachute Association approved school.
Price: Basingstoke £96, including hire of all equipment, and 1st jump. Leyland £85, excluding boots, overalls, but including 1st jump.

MOTOR RACING

Do you fancy yourself as a budding Niki Lauda?
Now's your chance to see if you've got the nerve for motor racing: take a 2-hour course of assessment at Silverstone Racing School. Drive either a race-prepared MG Maestro or a single-seater Formula Ford. The course is available at Oxford or Warwick. **Price:** £73

If you could afford it, or someone gave you the money, which would you choose? Why?
What sport (other than the two above) would you like to try? Why?
What sports are popular in your own country? Are there any 'new' sports?

and/or

4 *Work in groups of three. You are the committee responsible for organising an inter-college Sports Meeting. Today is 25th January: the sports meeting is set for 27th March.*
Below is the agenda giving details that must be decided at the committee meeting. Your teacher will tell you which item(s) you are responsible for. Make notes and be prepared to outline your suggestions to the rest of the committee (and to discuss the other items on the agenda).

INTER-COLLEGE SPORTS MEETING

Committee Meeting: 25th January

1 Venue and time: at one of the Colleges? Or on 'neutral ground'? Facilities that will be needed (e.g. changing rooms)? Morning? Afternoon? Or all day?
2 Publicity and advertising: only in colleges, or to general public? Free? Or charge for seats? (If so, price?) (Any prizes? If so, what, and how to purchase?)
3 Procedure for entries: production of entry forms, latest entry dates, etc. Any need for qualifying rounds? If so, in which events, and when and where?
4 Officials: recruit students and lecturers from different colleges? Or impartial outsiders from sports clubs?
5 Any other business.

Exam Three

PAPER 1: READING COMPREHENSION

Time: 1 hour

This paper is in two parts, Section A and Section B. For each question you answer correctly in Section A you gain one *mark; for each question you answer correctly in Section B you gain* two *marks. No marks are deducted for wrong answers. Answer all the questions. Indicate your choice of answer in every case on a separate sheet. Follow carefully the instructions about how to record your answers.*

Section A

In this Section you must choose the word or phrase which best completes each sentence. For each question, 1 to 25, **indicate on your answer sheet** *the letter A, B, C or D against the number of the question.*

1. According to a recent survey, most people are on good . . . . with their neighbours.
   A relations   B acquaintance   C relationships   D terms

2. That picture is somewhat . . . . of Picasso's early work.
   A mindful   B similar   C memorable   D reminiscent

3. The soap opera star threatened to . . . . her dentist for $10 million.
   A prosecute   B sue   C convict   D charge

4. There is a . . . . resemblance between the two of them.
   A striking   B piercing   C biting   D shining

5. I was in a quandary . . . . what to say.
   A for   B as to   C of   D owing to

6. At last he had found someone on whom he could vent his . . . .
   A anger   B love   C happiness   D trust

7. A boycott of other countries' sporting events appears a politically more expedient form of protest than trade . . . . against them.
   A treaties   B actions   C blocks   D sanctions

8. The low, unbroken . . . . of the machine next door gradually bored its way into his brain.
   A din   B thud   C blare   D hum

9. Some action groups have become so powerful that quite frequently we have a situation in which the tail wags the . . . .
   A cat   B body   C legs   D dog

10. Anyone is entitled to such benefit, ... of age or sex.
    A whether   B in spite   C in case   D regardless

11. The change in timetable will . . . . many students having to catch an earlier bus.
    A result   B lead   C mean   D cause

12 The ringleader was extremely lucky to get . . . . a suspended sentence.
    A away   B through to   C off with   D through

13 .. . . you aren't suggesting that what he did was in any way defensible?
    A Certainly   B Probably   C Undoubtedly   D Surely

14 Most prices have been . . . . in the final days of our clearance sale.
    A taken down   B diminished   C declined   D slashed

15 This curtain material . . . . easily.
    A hangs itself   B bends   C makes itself   D creases.

16 If . . . . in March, they should give you a host of splendid blooms a few months later.
    A installed   B earthed   C dug   D planted

17 Unfortunately it all . . . . to whether we can afford it.
    A boils down   B reduces   C sums up   D rings up

18 She is capable of . . . . sarcasm when she puts her mind to it.
    A striking   B sharpening   C slicing   D biting

19 We have been able to use these splendid premises this evening by . . . . of the Headmaster and governors.
    A courtesy   B thanks   C permission   D allowance

20 Those acting for the defendant propose to appeal . . . . the sentence.
    A to   B against   C for   D out

21 The doctors have doubtless done all they can; . . . . that's the impression I gained.
    A moreover   B at least   C nevertheless   D furthermore

22 Her political future is now hanging by a . . . .
    A rope   B cord   C string   D thread

23 I have no . . . . for self-opinionated people like him.
    A time   B interest   C care   D patience

24 . . . . regards sport and leisure activities, our two countries appear to have little in common.
    A How   B What   C As   D With

25 This is the last time I . . . . an exercise like this!
    A do   B did   C have done   D would do

Section B

In this Section you will find after each of the passages a number of questions or unfinished statements about the passage, each with four suggested answers or ways of finishing. You must choose the one which you think fits best. For each question, 26 to 40, **indicate on your answer sheet** *the letter A, B, C or D against the number of the question. Give* **one answer only** *to each question. Read each passage right through before choosing your answers.*

First passage

Chinese cinema is still the big unwritten chapter in world film history. The gap is surprising, if only because so many other facets of twentieth-century Chinese history, culture and politics have been extensively analysed. The past four years, however, have seen a significant growth of interest in Chinese film – both in China and farther afield. The China Film Archive, forced to close by Red Guards in 1966, resumed its activities in 1978; it has now recatalogued its collection and begun facing up to the massive task of copying its large holdings of old nitrate prints on to safety-film stock. Two years ago, it organised a retrospective season of pre-1949 films for internal circulation to film professionals in the country's leading production centres. This gave many of the younger film-makers their first glimpses of work done in the 1930s and 1940s. Later films, banned since the "anti-rightist purge" of 1957, have also begun to reappear on China's screens.

The belated western discovery of China's film heritage began at London's National Film Theatre in 1980, with a 25-film season called "Electric Shadows". (The exotic title was a literal translation of *dianying*, the Chinese word for "cinema".) Several classics had their first screenings outside China at this event, which established two important points. First, that the Shanghai film industry of the 1930s and 1940s produced work of international standing. Second, that the films of the People's Republic, while hardly as remarkable as their predecessors, did offer much more than celebrations of tractor maintenance and bayonet-wielding ballerinas.

The London initiative was quickly copied in a dozen or more cities, from Sydney to Turin, with the result that Chinese cinema has found a place on the map that it did not have in 1980. The decades of neglect and ignorance, however, have forced all such events to take the form of broad, general surveys, which has not helped the discovery of individual talents. It has also conveniently obscured underlying factors, like the Chinese willingness to supply certain titles and reluctance even to mention certain others.

London has now picked up the baton again with a second, larger season, to be held at the National Film Theatre throughout January and February. It is called, inevitably, "More Electric Shadows". Unlike the first season, this has been organised with the co-operation of the China Film Archive; the result is a programme more or less evenly balanced between pre-1949 and post-1949 titles. It offers more 1930s films than have previously been seen outside China at one time and includes a number of western premieres. The selection is doubtless no more coherent than previous ones, but it does add some missing pieces to the jigsaw.

26   In relation to our knowledge of 20th-century Chinese culture generally,
    A little is known about their films.
    B their cinemas are still an unknown quantity.
    C the actual history of the country is still somewhat hazy.
    D our growing interest is out of all proportion.

27   The retrospective season of pre-1949 films which was mentioned
    A was shown in cities all over the world.
    B consisted mainly of films banned since 1957.
    C was organised by the China Film Archive.
    D gave young film-makers a second chance to see films of the 30s and 40s.

28 The London season of 1980 proved that Chinese films of the People's Republic era
   A dealt solely with agricultural and martial themes.
   B were better than many Western films of the same era.
   C were inferior to the Shanghai 30s and 40s productions.
   D could rank among international film classics.

29 The writer seems to lament the fact that
   A too little has been done too late by the West.
   B some films have still not found their way out of China.
   C Western cinema-goers are still rather ignorant.
   D there are no individual talents in Chinese cinema.

30 The new season in January and February will be special because it will
   A show more films from the fifties.
   B include premieres of some Westerns.
   C be the second held in London.
   D be supported by the Chinese.

Second passage

I watched as Dr Ian Stead, the archaeologist in charge of the excavation, began carefully removing the peat with a clay modelling tool. X-rays taken through the box while it was at the hospital revealed ribs, backbone, arm bones and a skull (apparently with fractures). However, the bones showed up only faintly because acid in the peat had removed minerals from them.

Using the X-rays, Stead started on what he thought might be a leg. By his side was Professor Frank Oldfield, of Liverpool University, an expert on peat who could identify vegetation from stems only a fraction of an inch long.

"Similar bodies found in bogs in Denmark show signs of a violent death," Stead said. "It is essential for us to be able to distinguish between the plant fibres in peat and clothing or a piece of rope which might have been used to hang him."

Occasionally, Oldfield would pop a small piece of peat in his mouth to clean it and then, examining it with a magnifying glass, would pronounce upon the species. "Cranberry stems in the peat around the body suggest that it lay in a pool of water," he said. "Then the pool gradually silted up, cotton sedge grew in it, and finally heather grew on top of the body, forming a hummock."

As Stead continued his gentle probing, a brown leathery limb began to materialise amidst the peat; but not until most of it was exposed could he and Robert Connolly, a physical anthropologist at Liverpool University, decide that it was an arm. Beside it was a small piece of animal fur – perhaps the remains of clothing.

Following the forearm down into the peat, Stead found a brown shiny object and then, close by, two more. At first they looked like hazel nuts. Seen under a magnifying glass, though, he suddenly realised they were fingernails – "beautifully manicured and without a scratch on them," he said.

"Most people at this time in the Iron Age were farmers; but with fingernails like that, this person can't have been. He might have been a priest or an aristocrat."

Especially delicate work was required to reveal the head. On the third day, a curly sideburn appeared and, shortly afterwards, a moustache. At first it seemed that the man had been balding but gradually he was seen to have close-cropped hair, about an inch or two long. "The hair was probably cut with a razor or shears – scissors were not invented until later," Stead said.

"This information about his hairstyle is unique. We have no other information about what Britons looked like before the Roman invasion except for three small plaques showing Celts with drooping moustaches and shaven chins."

The crucial clue showing how the man died had already been revealed, close to his neck, but it looked just like another innocent heather root. It was not recognised until two days later, when Margaret McCord, a senior conservation officer, found the same root at the back of his neck and, cleaning it carefully, saw its twisted texture. "He's been garrotted." she declared.

The 'root' was a length of twisted sinew, the thickness of strong string. A slip knot at the back shows how it was tightened round the neck.

"A piece of stick was probably inserted and the thong twisted round to throttle him." Stead said, "A large discoloration on the left shoulder suggests a bruise and possibly a violent struggle."

31 The X-rays that were taken told Stead and Oldfield
    A less than they would have liked.
    B exactly what to look for.
    C which deposits were clay and which peat.
    D exactly how the man had died.

32 The researchers suspected the man had met a violent death because
    A he was still wearing clothes.
    B similar bodies had been found in bogs in Denmark.
    C there were traces of a hanging rope in the peat.
    D he hadn't been buried in a coffin.

33 It was the first limb they uncovered which
    A required the most delicate work.
    B indicated the age of the man.
    C told them something about the man's clothes.
    D led them to discover the fingernails.

34 Why did the researchers think the man was possibly a priest?
    A He had closely-cropped hair.
    B His hair was curly at the sides.
    C He had a drooping moustache and shaven chin.
    D His fingernails were well looked after.

35 It was established that the man they dug out of the peat had been
    A beheaded.
    B strangled.
    C suffocated.
    D stabbed in the neck.

Third passage

Grammar, spelling, and punctuation should be brought back to the forefront in teaching English to school pupils, according to a consultative document published today by the Schools Inspectorate.

The document, *English from Five to Sixteen*, sets the pattern for agreed objectives in English teaching for the first time in British state education. In the document the inspectors outline a rigorous programme of targets for all pupils in two of the three Rs: reading and writing.

The document says: "If a basic level of literacy and articulateness is not attained by the age of seven, it becomes very difficult to achieve competence in other learning, much of which relies on the ability to read, to discuss, and to record in writing."

The consultative document is the first in a number of similar proposals to be published by the Department of Education and Science during the next few months.

MILESTONES IN ENGLISH

The inspectors suggest that the pupils should have achieved the following at each stage of their school career:

By the age of 7

Listening: Carry out simple, heard instructions; understand simple oral information; keep listening attentively for reasonably lengthy periods; follow and remember an uncomplicated story; respond to poetic rhythm.

Speaking: Speak clearly and audibly; narrate events; explain what they are doing; discuss with other children; express feelings to adults; ask relevant questions; describe what they have seen; converse confidently.

Reading: Understand labels, notices, and written instructions; read simple stories, rhymes, information passages; know the alphabet, consult dictionaries; enjoy books; use books as information sources.

Writing: Be able to write legibly; write personal experience in prose and poetry; link writing to pictures, graphs, and plans; record investigations; write simple stories and informal letters, descriptions, directions.

By the age of 11

All pupils should be able to embark on secondary schooling "without hindrance or handicap" in linguistic ability.

Listening: Hear fairly complex instructions, and carry them out; follow story plots or broadcast plays; respond to poetry.

Speaking: Speak with expression and sensitivity to listener's response; show some ability to match vocabulary, syntax and style to various situations; converse confidently and pleasantly; frame pertinent questions.

Reading: Have formed the habit of voluntary and sustained reading for pleasure and information; know how to find books in library.

Writing: Describe personal feelings, thoughts, and experiences; produce vivid imaginative writing, accurate recording, persuasive writing, formal letters; have control over syntax, and good handwriting.

About Language: Rules of spelling; vowels and consonants, nouns, pronouns, verbs, adjectives, adverbs, statements, questions, commands, exclamations, subject and object, and tenses; should all be used and understood.

Detailed answers and marking schemes

Exam One

PAPER 1: READING COMPREHENSION
(pages 2–8)

Answer Key

Section A
1 C; 2 A; 3 D; 4 A; 5 B; 6 C; 7 D; 8 A;
9 B; 10 A; 11 B; 12 C; 13 D; 14 A; 15 C;
16 A; 17 B; 18 D; 19 A; 20 D; 21 B; 22 B;
23 A; 24 D; 25 C

Section B
First passage: 26 B; 27 D; 28 A; 29 C; 30 C
Second passage: 31 C; 32 D; 33 B; 34 D; 35 C
Third passage: 36 B; 37 A; 38 B; 39 D; 40 B

Suggested marking scheme

Section A
25 items, 1 mark for each correct answer   25

Section B
15 items, 2 marks for each correct answer   30

Possible maximum total for the whole Paper: 55

PAPER 2: COMPOSITION
(page 9)

Suggested marking scheme

Use an impression mark to assess the compositions (each out of a possible total of 20), taking the following factors into account:
- the quality and naturalness of the language employed.
- the range and appropriateness of vocabulary and sentence structure.
- the correctness of grammar, punctuation and spelling.
- the relevance and organisation of the compositions.
- length requirements.

The University of Cambridge Local Examinations Syndicate has published the following table to show how the impression mark is given at Proficiency level:

18–20	Excellent	Error-free, substantial and varied material, resourceful and controlled in language and expression.
16–17	Very good	Good realistion of task, ambitious and natural in style.
12–15	Good	Sufficient assurance and freedom from basic error to maintain theme.
8–11	Pass	Clear realisation of task, reasonably correct and natural.
5–7	Weak	Near to pass level in general scope, but with either numerous errors or too elementary or translated in style.
0–4	Very poor	Basic errors, narrowness of vocabulary.

The Syndicate interprets these marks as follows:
40% of the total (ie 8 out of 20) – rough pass
60% – good pass
75%–90% – a very good standard

PAPER 3: USE OF ENGLISH
(pages 10–13)

Answer Key

Section A

1 1 spite; 2 which/that; 3 someone/somebody/him/her; 4 before/over/at; 5 only/just; 6 usually/generally/always/invariably; 7 yet; 8 what; 9 be; 10 for/in; 11 would; 12 which; 13 as; 14 to; 15 has/had/needed; 16 as/that; 17 had; 18 them; 19 as/since/because; 20 since/ago

2 a) If I hadn't lost my passport last week, I wouldn't be having so much trouble now.
b) The police caught him (as he was) climbing over the garden wall.
c) Sad though/as it is, unemployment is unlikely to go down this year.
d) The man is believed to have escaped in a stolen car.
e) Having nothing else to do, we decided to go for a walk.
f) She flatly refused to sleep in the/that haunted house.
g) They didn't need to/They didn't have to call for help after all.
h) Nowhere will you find a more dedicated worker than Mrs Jones.

3 a) started *or* should have finished
b) did I realise/understand
c) poorly/badly attended was *or* few people came to/attended
d) wanting/wishing to register *or* who wish to register/who are planning to register
e) best not/better not *or* be wise not to
f) had (already) eaten/had finished eating

4 a) I don't want to be disturbed.
b) He took the company to court on the grounds that he had been unfairly dismissed *or* because he felt he had been unfairly dismissed.
c) There's every likelihood/chance/possibility (that) we'll be late.
d) The Committee's preference was for the first proposal. *or* The Committee expressed a preference for the first proposal.
e) I really must get down to answering all these letters.
f) Don't blame yourself./You mustn't blame yourself./You're not to blame.
g) There's quite a lot of criticism directed at the police nowadays./The police seem to be attracting (*or* coming in for) quite a lot of criticism nowadays.
h) Putting it bluntly/Put bluntly/Quite bluntly/To put it bluntly/Bluntly, the man's an idiot!

Section B

5 Answers to questions a)–n) may well be worded differently to the following suggested answers, but the information and ideas they contain should be the same.

a) It had mistaken its own reflection for a rival bird.
b) The bird was part of an experiment which they had instigated and were supervising.
c) They are being steadily poisoned by DDT, a chemical which makes their eggs too fragile.
d) He tries to make the bird sound almost human, 'dine' being almost exclusively used for people; it also implies a select diet.
e) Makes with difficulty from bits and pieces scratched from the ground.
f) City pigeons would not have the toxic chemicals in them that Californian country birds have.
g) It regained consciousness just in time to fly up again instead of being smashed against the ground.
h) Helicopters.
i) They are sufficiently clever and cunning to find food in the city.
j) They were pleased at the sight of four eggs in the falcon's nest, worried when two were destroyed.
k) They stay close to the ground.
l) Covered with the remains of people's meals.
m) The city pigeons were too clever for them, so the peregrines could only catch migrating birds, poisoned with DDT.
n) They adopted them and treated them as their own.
o) Possible summary:
An endangered species because of the DDT they are being poisoned with through their food, peregrine falcons have been brought into Los Angeles and encouraged to feed off uncontaminated city pigeons. They are observed and at times actively assisted with their breeding by ornithologists. The falcons have adapted well, have learnt to avoid danger and have developed effective hunting tactics. However, the urban pigeons' defensive tactics have also improved and the peregrines are being forced to eat contaminated migratory birds. The problem of their over-fragile, DDT-infected eggs, therefore, is still to be solved, and the future is uncertain.

Suggested marking scheme

Section A
1   20 items, 1 mark each   20
2   8 sentences, 2 marks each   16
3   6 sentences, 2 marks each   12
4   8 sentences, 2 marks each   16

Possible total maximum: 64

Section B
14 questions (a–n), 3 marks each   42
Summary (question o)   24

Possible total maximum: 66

Possible maximum total for
the whole Paper: 130

Allotment of marks

In Section A **2**, **3** and **4**, award half marks for partially correct sentences.

In Section B questions (a)–(n), answers should be coherent, relevant and in correct English. Award half marks where appropriate.

In Section B question (o), the summary should be well-expressed and contain all and only the relevant information. Allot marks accordingly.

PAPER 4: LISTENING COMPREHENSION
(pages 14—16)

Tapescript   (See pages 72–75)

Answer Key

First part
1 False; 2 True; 3 False; 4 True; 5 True; 6 False; 7 True

Second part
8 2/only a couple of places (*not* 12); 9 half board (*not* full board); 10 £410 (*not* £210); 11 March (*not* April); 12 not a 'first class hotel'; 13 telephone number wrong – should be 429870 (*not* 429807)

Third Part
14 C; 15 B; 16 B; 17 D; 18 A

Fourth part
19 D; 20 D; 21 B; 22 D; 23 D; 24 A

Suggested marking scheme
24 items, 1 mark each   24
Possible total maximum for the
   whole Paper: 24

PAPER 5: INTERVIEW
(pages 17–18)

2   Passage **i)** is most probably from a newspaper report or from a news report read on radio or television. Passage **ii)** is almost certainly a piece of spoken English, although it could be from a personal letter to a friend.

Exam Two

PAPER 1: READING COMPREHENSION
(pages 19—25)

Answer Key

Section A
1 A; 2 B; 3 B; 4 C; 5 B; 6 C; 7 C; 8 A; 9 B; 10 B; 11 D; 12 C; 13 A; 14 D; 15 A; 16 B; 17 A; 18 C; 19 D; 20 C; 21 D; 22 C; 23 C; 24 B; 25 D

Section B
First passage: 26 B; 27 A; 28 A; 29 B; 30 C
Second passage: 31 B; 32 D; 33 A; 34 C; 35 D
Third passage: 36 C; 37 A; 38 C; 39 D; 40 C

Suggested marking scheme
See the scheme suggested for Exam One, Paper 1

PAPER 2: COMPOSITION
(page 26)

See the suggested marking scheme for Exam One, Paper 2

PAPER 3: USE OF ENGLISH
(pages 27–30)

Answer Key

Section A

1 1 hardly/scarcely/barely; 2 little/nothing; 3 seems/appears; 4 over; 5 Throughout/During; 6 Although/Though; 7 where; 8 must/should/could; 9 later/then/went; 10 becoming; 11 have/get; 12 was; 13 to; 14 as; 15 by/in; 16 that; 17 extending/broadening; 18 put/bring; 19 the; 20 whose

2 a) Hardly had she begun to speak before/when people started interrupting her.
b) Getting into work this morning was a bit difficult.
c) Much to our regret, we have to/must/are obliged to inform you that your application has not been successful.
d) There's very little/not a lot/hardly anything he doesn't know about whales.
e) The sooner we (can) solve the problem, the better it will be for all concerned.
f) So great was the demand that they had to reprint the book immediately.
g) They can't (possibly) have been playing in this weather.
h) He denied stealing/having stolen/that he had stolen the car, but admitted borrowing/having borrowed/that he had borrowed it.

3 a) (went and) had/got it cut/trimmed *or* had a haircut *or* did something about it *or* went to the hairdresser('s)/barber('s)
b) had been looking/had been paying attention to/had known (exactly)
c) (rather), worked/did work/did/used to (work)
d) to/to doing/to having to do/to being asked to do/to being told to do
e) were having/must have been having
f) will she suspect *or* does she know

4 a) I (just) can't wait to meet them.
b) They spent the whole week lying on the beach sunbathing.
c) I have serious doubts as to whether this will work.
d) He's always had great difficulty in learning English.
e) I don't/do not intend to give up now.
f) They've always had/been given/been allowed the/complete freedom to do what they want.
g) This (sort of thing) happens/occurs quite frequently.
h) I was sorely tempted to say exactly what I thought.

Section B

5 Answers to questions a)–n) may well be worded differently to the following suggested answers, but the information and ideas they contain should be the same.

a) Child prodigies nowadays can create all manner of problems, particularly for their parents.
b) A reading aloud in a high-pitched voice.
c) The young child's genius was discovered quite late and caused embarrassment; the 13-year-old's was identified sooner, was coached and encouraged.
d) She has had an extraordinary education from a very young age and never attended normal school.
e) It could make her emotionally and psychologically unstable, causing loneliness and feelings of isolation.
f) 'Vaulted' is much more dramatic than 'jumped' or 'skipped', suggesting a higher leap.
g) Other prodigies in the field of mathematics have shown a similar rate of progress.
h) Their creative powers slow down and go into relative decline.
i) They are appreciated and therefore encouraged more by adults because in some respects they may be more advanced than grown-ups.
j) They are children who have been given jobs in an adult world because of their exceptional talents.
k) Employed with a salary.
l) Literature is usually a subject which relies on a mature, adult consciousness and awareness of the world about us.
m) It can create anxiety in parents.
n) Mothers who want to push their children into show business as actors, singers, etc. even if the children themselves show little ability or talent.
o) Points:
– child prodigies not always a blessing; sometimes a liability to parents and source of embarrassment
– some cases spotted early, others discovered relatively late and by chance
– examples of children 'vaulting' years at school
– examples of children being employed at a very young age
– dangers of loneliness and isolation through not being with other children
– mathematics, music and computers: areas in which prodigies most appreciated by adults

Suggested marking scheme and allotment of marks

See the suggested marking scheme and allotment of marks for Exam One, Paper 3.

PAPER 4: LISTENING COMPREHENSION
(pages 31–34)

Tapescript (See pages 75–78)

Answer Key

First part
1 D; 2 D; 3 B; 4 A; 5 C

Second part
6 Mr & Mrs V.J. Gyles; 7 American; 8 0904 40068; 9 Double room with shower; 10 30/4–1/5; 11 £35

Third part

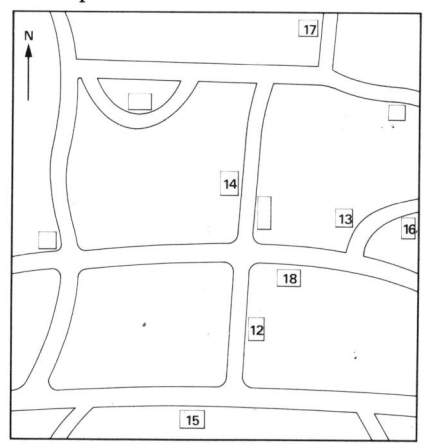

Fourth part
19 4; 20 2; 21 5; 22 1; 23 6; 24 3; 25 9; 26 7; 27 8

Suggested marking scheme
27 items, 1 mark each ___27___

Possible total maximum for the
 whole Paper: ___27___

PAPER 5: INTERVIEW
(pages 35–36)

2 Passage **i)** is most probably from an advertisement on radio or television or from an advertisement in a newspaper or magazine. Passage **ii)** is almost certainly an extract from a rule book about hockey.

Exam Three
PAPER 1: READING COMPREHENSION
(pages 37–43)

Answer Key

Section A
1 D; 2 D; 3 B; 4 A; 5 B; 6 A; 7 D; 8 D;
9 D; 10 D; 11 C; 12 C; 13 D; 14 D; 15 D;
16 D; 17 A; 18 D; 19 A; 20 B; 21 B; 22 D;
23 A; 24 C; 25 A

Section B
First passage: 26 A; 27 C; 28 C; 29 B; 30 D
Second passage: 31 A; 32 B; 33 D; 34 D; 35 B
Third passage: 36 D; 37 C; 38 C; 39 D; 40 B

Suggested marking scheme
See the scheme suggested for Exam One, Paper 1.

PAPER 2: COMPOSITION
(page 44)

See the suggested marking scheme for Exam One, Paper 2.

PAPER 3: USE OF ENGLISH
(pages 45–48)

Answer Key

Section A
1 1 advising/urging/inviting/recommending; 2 even; 3 Should; 4 wherever; 5 Thus/So; 6 with; 7 could/would; 8 safe/secure/happy/content; 9 would/could/(might); 10 attracting; 11 by; 12 such/these/most/their; 13 Simply/Just; 14 in; 15 were/was; 16 dare; 17 say; 18 somewhat/very/rather/highly/extremely/most, 19 however/though; 20 being

2 a) If I had (only) been thinking, I wouldn't have made that terrible mistake.
b) We were planning/going/intending to visit/ We were to visit grandmother, so we left early in the morning.
c) No sooner had the burglars left the building than someone rang the alarm.
d) The more popular television programmes become, the worse they seem to get.

e) He dismissed the whole idea as (being) ridiculous.
f) Anyone found trespassing on this land will be prosecuted (by the authorities).
g) I'd rather go out for a meal than stay at home.
h) But for the weather, it would have been a super weekend./the weekend would have been super.

3 a) must/should/may you tell *or* talk to/tell (i.e. *simple imperative*)
b) Have you been
c) it not been for
d) will have been/will have lived/will have been living
e) her going out/staying out/coming home/being out

4 a) I was led to believe the film would be very good.
b) She made/offered her apologies, and left early.
c) The deadline for registration is 1st April.
d) The refugees badly need warm clothes./Warm clothes are badly needed by the refugees.
e) I found the whole thing baffling.
f) You are under no obligation to buy one if you don't like it.
g) As long as/So long as you promise not to laugh, I'll show you our holiday snaps.
h) What do you think the outcome of the present negotiations will be?/What do you think will be the outcome of the present negotiations?

Section B

5 Answers to questions a)–n) may well be worded differently to the following suggested answers, but the information and ideas they contain should be the same.

a) By small highspeed pieces of rock and metal from space.
b) Fragments and matter that come from outside the earth's atmosphere.
c) Meteorites actually arrive on earth whereas meteors are vaporised before they can reach us.
d) Turned from solid into a gas or moisture.
e) They give off a very bright light.
f) Small drops of melted metal iron have been seen on fresh snow.
g) Not as one would expect or as would be normal.
h) People believed that spacecraft would be seriously damaged by the host of meteorites falling through space.
i) Normally associated with rain, this expression suggests a dense and continuous shower.
j) Collision with another astronomical body or a 'black hole'.
k) Even small bodies could affect the earth's surface and create conditions in which we could not survive.
l) Very unfavourable or damaging to life as we know it at present.
m) Asteroids, comets from within our Solar System, large astronomical bodies, dust clouds and streams of meteorite matter from outside.
n) Such collisions have already occurred in the distant past (according to statistical estimates).
o) Points for summary:
– meteorites: many survive entry into our atmosphere and reach the ground – have been found inside buildings as well as outside
– Possibility of collision with large astronomical body or 'black hole' – even a near-miss could be disastrous
– small extraterrestrial bodies might affect our earth's surface on impact detrimentally
– danger of dust clouds and possibly large streams of meteorite matter
– from within our Solar System, asteroids and comets; it's suggested that this kind of collision does happen

Suggested marking scheme and allotment of marks

See the suggested marking scheme and allotment of marks for Exam One, Paper 3

PAPER 4: LISTENING COMPREHENSION
(pages 49–51)

Tapescript (See pages 79–82)

Answer Key

First part
1 D; 2 C; 3 A; 4 C; 5 B

Second part
6 B; 7 A; 8 B; 9 C; 10 D; 11 B

Third part
12 False; 13 True; 14 True; 15 True; 16 False; 17 False; 18 True; 19 False

Fourth part

SCORECARD		
Balsover Fliers	Malvern Mounties	Compere
ROUND THREE		
20 1906	—	1905
21 1926	1930	—
22 1911	—	1912
23 1899	1896	1886
ROUND FOUR		
24 The Golden Arrow	The Sunbeam	—
25 Crane manufacturer	Mechanic	—
26 —	A lord	—
27 —	'A'	—

Suggested marking scheme

27 items, 1 mark each   27

Possible total maximum for the
   whole Paper: 27

PAPER 5: INTERVIEW
(pages 52–53)

2   Passage **i)** is most probably from an article in a serious magazine or from a book about the subject of animal rights. It is certainly formal written English. Passage **ii)** is certainly spoken English, most probably spoken to a friend, but could be transcribed from an interview about holidays.

Exam Four

PAPER 1: READING COMPREHENSION
(pages 54–60)

Answer Key

Section A
1 C; 2 A; 3 C; 4 A; 5 B; 6 B; 7 A; 8 D;
9 C; 10 D; 11 A; 12 D; 13 B; 14 D; 15 D;
16 C; 17 C; 18 A; 19 C; 20 A; 21 D; 22 C;
23 C; 24 A; 25 D

Section B
First passage: 26 D; 27 A; 28 C; 29 D; 30 B
Second passage: 31 B; 32 A; 33 C; 34 A; 35 B
Third passage: 36 B; 37 D; 38 B; 39 B; 40 C

Suggested marking scheme
See the scheme suggested for Exam One, Paper 1.

PAPER 2: COMPOSITION
(page 61)
See the suggested marking scheme for Exam One, Paper 2.

PAPER 3: USE OF ENGLISH
(pages 62–65)

Answer Key

Section A
1   1 has; 2 as; 3 enough; 4 apart/aside;
5 associated/connected; 6 today/do/already;
7 from; 8 on; 9 though/although/albeit;
10 than; 11 all; 12 where; 13 eventually/soon/ undoubtedly/inevitably; 14 which; 15 for;
16 by; 17 having; 18 so/more/fully/ completely/totally; 19 in; 20 wonders

2   a) The team leader criticised John for not waiting/for not having waited for them.
b) He might not have got my letter.
c) It last snowed here six years ago./It hasn't snowed here for six years./It was six years ago that/when it last snowed here.
d) Only when they told me about it later did I realise what I had missed.
e) There were far fewer people there than I had expected.
f) On being asked about the strike, the Minister declined to comment.
g) You needn't have gone to all that trouble./ You didn't need to go to all that trouble.
h) I wish you wouldn't say things like that.

3   a) would have been
b) always telling
c) should/ought to have come/gone
d) I've been wanting/hoping
e) to be congratulated
f) to have been born

4   a) I'd rather you waited until they bring/ brought out a new model.
b) The cat was nowhere to be found./Nowhere could the cat be found./Nowhere could we find the cat.

c) What finally ended the dispute was the union's agreement to go to arbitration./The union's agreement to go to arbitration was what finally ended the dispute.
d) He objects to anyone else touching/He objects if anyone else touches his records.
e) What surprised me was (the fact) that nobody said anything at the time./The fact that nobody said anything at the time was what surprised me.
f) They had been playing for 30 minutes when the referee first blew his whistle.
g) I took the blame for burning/having burnt the toast./I admitted I was to blame for burning/having burnt the toast.
h) The upkeep of the museum is becoming extremely expensive.

Section B
5 Answers to questions a)–m) may well be worded differently to the following suggested answers, but the information and ideas they contain should be the same.

a) It illustrates a very unusual and unlikely invention that someone might want a patent for.
b) 'Boffins' (*slang*) are technicians or scientists engaged in some kind of research. 'Garden shed' indicates that they are amateurs working from home.
c) To ensure that for the next 20 years no one can steal one's idea and make a profit from it.
d) Moving along in a crowd, like a herd of cattle.
e) We are told it is an anonymous-looking building, so it obviously does not stand out as a landmark.
f) There are countless ants in an ant heap, all engaged in furious activity. The implication here is that the Patent Office is an extremely crowded and busy building.
g) The particular inventions that each individual has come up with.
h) Because the patents for both are filed in the Patent Office.
i) He was the first person to be granted an official patent.
j) A more complicated, less straightforward business.
k) It is extremely difficult. Strict procedures are laid down and the whole business takes time and money, not to mention a little luck.
l) Reduces to one word; puts in a nutshell.
m) It must show inventiveness and ingenuity on the part of the inventor.
n) Possible Summary:
One major problem in obtaining a patent is the huge number of applications received by the Patent Office in London. One is in competition with up to 40,000 other inventors every year. The bureaucratic procedures are now very complex and time-consuming. One may expect to have to wait two and a half years and the cost may be £165. Additionally, one needs luck and an invention which can boast originality and ingenuity.

Suggested marking scheme and allotment of marks

See the suggested marking scheme and the allotment of marks for Exam One, Paper 3.

PAPER 4: LISTENING COMPREHENSION
(pages 66–69)

Tapescript (See pages 83–86)

Answer Key

First part
1 False; 2 False; 3 False; 4 True; 5 False; 6 True; 7 False; 8 True; 9 False; 10 True

Second part
11 C; 12 A; 13 B

Third part
14 Tea; 15 Chewing-gum; 16 Candlewax; 17 Milk; 18 Shoe polish

Fourth part
19 B; 20 A; 21 D; 22 B; 23 A

Fifth part
24 A; 25 D; 26 B; 27 B; 28 A

Suggested marking scheme

28 items, 1 mark each	28
Possible total maximum for the whole Paper:	28

PAPER 5: INTERVIEW
(pages 70–71)

2 Passage **i)** is almost certainly a piece of spoken English, possibly transcribed from an interview with an older person. (It could of course be from a letter to a newspaper or magazine.) Passage **ii)** is quite formal written English, and is from a leaflet advertising adult education college courses.

By the age of 16

Listening: Understand instructions of length and complexity; demonstrate ability to concentrate on oral discussion, taking notes; criticize attempts to persuade listener, "so as to recognize specious arguments and loaded language".

Speaking: Discuss cooperatively in groups to reach agreed outcomes; argue a case; be able to accommodate the language limitations of others; be able to elucidate, amplify, or rephrase what others say; give short talks.

Reading: Read full range of literature, whole long books; read newspapers and advertising critically, distinguish bias, criticize television and reporting; show ability to judge quality and value.

Writing: Explore and conclude issues; use stylistic effects; use direct and reported speech; write job application letters and curricula vitae.

About language: Know all the main parts of speech, including prepositions and conjunctions; use formal and informal styles; show knowledge of metaphor, simile, and cliché; demonstrate proper use of figurative language.

36 *English from Five to Sixteen* is setting a precedent in that
  A it focusses attention on pupils' reading and writing skills.
  B it excludes arithmetic, conventionally the third 'R'.
  C in it, traditional grammar comes before everything else.
  D no other such document has ever been published in Britain.

37 According to the document, which of these should an 11-year-old have developed?
  A The skill of recording his or her own speech.
  B A facility for literary appreciation.
  C A feeling for tone and appropriacy in speech.
  D A critical faculty in reading.

38 Which of these would a 7-year-old be expected to do?
  A Read for long periods for enjoyment.
  B Understand the rules of grammar.
  C Use certain reference books.
  D Write and persuade someone to do something.

39 By 16, a student should long ago have
  A read extensively in classical literature.
  B studied figures of speech.
  C got used to presenting short lectures to an audience.
  D learned to influence a reader with his or her written English.

40 The document says that the 16-year-old listener should be able to
  A concentrate on everything he or she listens to.
  B see through hollow reasoning.
  C answer clichés with clichés.
  D write down accurately everything he or she hears.

PAPER 2: COMPOSITION

Time: 2 hours

Write **two only** *of the following composition exercises. Your answers must follow exactly the instructions given. Write in pen, not pencil. You are allowed to make alterations, but see that your work is clear and easy to read.*

1. 'Dieting, keeping fit and so on are all right, but people are taking them to extremes.' Write a balanced discussion on this theme. (About 350 words)

2. Describe the achievements and influence of any historical figure. (About 300 words)

3. Write an account of one day in your life that you will never forget. (About 350 words)

4. A report in a recent consumer magazine gave the following criteria by which to judge a moped. (A moped is a motorcycle with a very low-powered motor, which frequently has to be pedal-assisted to start.) In a letter to the magazine (about 250 words), write an account of your experiences with a particular moped which you think meets most of the criteria and which you would recommend. You do not need to add addresses, etc. Simply begin: 'Dear Sir, . . .'

● Performance:	should be easy to start; engine should perform smoothly.
● Handling:	should ride well and not wobble: foot-rests should not touch road when cornering.
● Braking:	should operate well in all conditions: look for foot-operated as well as hand brakes on some models.
● Comfort:	seat comfortable and with height adjustment? handlebars right distance from seat? moped well-sprung?
● Convenience:	should be easy to fill with fuel; stand easy to use? should have container(s) for shopping, etc.
● Controls, lights and horn:	all controls (speedometer, etc.) easy to read? should have good headlight, brake light and indicators; could a pedestrian hear the horn in heavy traffic?
● Economy:	you should get about 120 miles per gallon; a full tank should take you about 75 miles.
● Maintenance:	how easy is it to do repairs? e.g. easy to remove wheels, get to the battery, etc? tools provided?

5. *(This will be a choice of questions on the prescribed texts.)*

Exam Three

PAPER 3: USE OF ENGLISH

Time: 2 hours

Section A

1 *Fill each of the numbered blanks in the following passage with* **one** *suitable word.*

I have just read an advertisement .... (1) me to purchase a new cordless telephone – 'You can pop it in your briefcase or .... (2) in a large coat pocket. .... (3) the people in your office need to contact you, they can do so .... (4) you may be.' .... (5) ran the ad.

The whole business fills me .... (6) utter dread!

In the Golden Days before The Telephone, a person .... (7) go and do his day's labour and then retire to his home, ... (8) in the knowledge that the only people who .... (9) bother him would be his neighbours or relatives. Even then, because the only way of .... (10) his attention was .... (11) banging on the door, knocking the door knocker or perhaps ringing the bell, a person could ignore .... (12) intrusions. But not now! Oh, no! .... (13) by dialling your number, a stranger can .... (14) effect walk into your house as if he .... (15) walking in through an open front door!

I hardly .... (16) think of the situations or geographical locations I might be in where the ringing of the cordless telephone would be, to .... (17) the least, ... (18) embarrassing.

I have, ... (19), just had a morbid last thought in its favour. For anyone afraid of .... (20) buried alive, the thought of the inclusion of a cordless telephone in the coffin might well provide much-needed consolation.

2 *Finish each of the following sentences in such a way that it means exactly the same as the sentence printed before it.*

Example: The gateway was too narrow for me to drive the car through.
Answer: The gateway wasn't *wide enough for me to drive the car through.*

a) I only made that terrible mistake because I wasn't thinking.
   If I ....

b) We had planned to visit grandmother, so we left early in the morning.
   We were ....

c) Someone rang the alarm as soon as the burglars left the building.
   No sooner ....

d) As television programmes become more popular, they seem to get worse.
   The more ....

e) 'I think the whole idea's ridiculous,' he said.
   He dismissed ....

f) The authorities will prosecute anyone they find trespassing on this land.
   Anyone found ....

g) I prefer going out for a meal to staying at home.
   I'd rather ....

h) It would have been a super weekend if it hadn't been for the weather.
   But ....

3 *Fill each of the blanks with a suitable word or phrase.*

Example: 1 *had already put* the letter in the letterbox when I realised that I had forgotten to put a stamp on it.

a) Under no circumstances . . . . anyone about the plans until they have been announced officially. And that's an order.

b) '. . . . . to the bank today?'
'Oh, no. But there's still time. They don't close until half past three.'

c) Had . . . . for the fact that my wife was in the show, I would have walked out halfway through.

d) By next year my parents . . . . in the same house for forty years.

e) When she was younger, Jane's parents objected to . . . . late at night.

4 *For each of the sentences below, write a new sentence as similar as possible in meaning to the original sentence, but using the words given: these words* **must not be altered** *in any way.*

Example: She made sure everyone knew she was there.
   presence
Answer: She made her presence felt.

a) I was told the film would be very good.
   led
   ....

b) She apologised for having to go so early, and left.
   apologies
   ....

c) You have to register by 1st April at the latest.
   deadline
   ....

d) The refugees are in serious need of warm clothes.
   badly
   ....

e) I was mystified by the whole thing.
   baffling
   ....

f) You don't have to buy one if you don't like it.
   obligation
   ....

g) If you promise not to laugh, I'll show you our holiday snaps.
   long
   ....

h) How do you think the present negotiations will turn out?
   outcome
   ....

Section B

5 *Read the following passage, then answer the questions which follow it.*

Every day of our lives we are in danger of instant death from small high-speed missiles from space – the lumps of rocky or metallic extraterrestrial debris which continuously bombard the Earth. The chances of anyone actually being hit, however, are very low, although there are recorded instances of 'stones from the sky' hurting people, and numerous accounts of damage to buildings and other objects. At night this extraterrestrial material can be seen as 'fireballs' or 'shooting stars', burning their way through our atmosphere. If they survive their fiery entry into the Earth's atmosphere so that some part of their solid substance reaches the ground they are termed *meteorites*: most, on reaching our atmosphere, become completely vaporised and scientists call these *meteors*.

The height above ground at which these objects become sufficiently heated to be visible is estimated to be about 60–100 miles. An iron meteor as small as the head of a pin can shine with a light equal to that of a bright star. Surfaces of fresh snow have sometimes been seen to be covered with minute drops of melted metal iron after a group of shooting stars has crossed the sky. Meteorites that have fallen on buildings have sometimes ended their long lonely space voyage incongruously under beds, inside flower pots or even, in the case of one that landed on a hotel in North Wales, within a chamber pot. Before the era of space exploration it was confidently predicted that neither men nor space vehicles would survive for long outside the protective blanket of the Earth's atmosphere. It was thought that once in space they would be seriously damaged as a result of the incessant downpour of meteorites falling towards our planet at the rate of many millions every day. Even the first satellites showed that the danger from meteorites had been greatly overestimated by the pessimists, but although it has not happened yet, it is certain that one day a spacecraft will be badly damaged by a meteorite.

The greatest single potential danger to life on Earth undoubtedly comes from outside our planet. Collision with another astronomical body of any size or with a 'black hole' could completely destroy the Earth almost instantly. Near misses of bodies larger than or comparable in size to our own planet could be equally disastrous to mankind as they might still result in total or partial disruption. If the velocity of impact were high, collision with even quite small extraterrestrial bodies might cause catastrophic damage to the Earth's atmosphere, oceans and outer crust and thus produce results inimical to life as we know it. The probability of collision with a large astronomical body from outside our Solar System is extremely low, possibly less than once in the lifetime of an average star. We know, however, that our galaxy contains great interstellar dust clouds and some astronomers have suggested that there might also be immense streams of meteorite matter in space that the Solar System may occasionally encounter. Even if we disregard this possibility, our own Solar System itself contains a great number of small astronomical bodies, such as the minor planets or asteroids and the comets, some with eccentric orbits that occasionally bring them close to the Earth's path. While there are considerable difficulties in assessing the likelihood of a collision between the Earth and one of the larger comets or asteroids with any degree of accuracy, the statistical estimates that have been made certainly suggest that collisions of this kind do happen and, indeed, were extremely frequent during the early history of the Earth.

a) According to the writer, the Earth is being 'continuously bombarded'. By what?

b) Explain in your own words 'extraterrestrial debris' (line 2).

c) What is the difference between meteorites and meteors?

d) Explain the phrase 'completely vaporised' (line 9).

e) Why can even minute meteors and meteorites be seen in the sky?

f) What evidence of shooting stars passing over has sometimes been found on earth?

g) Explain in your own words the word 'incongruously' (line 16).

h) Why was it once thought that no spacecraft would survive for very long in space?

i) Explain the phrase 'the incessant downpour' (line 21).

j) What, according to the writer, is the greatest danger to life on Earth?

k) In what way(s) could collision with a small extraterrestrial body be fatal for us?

l) Explain the phrase 'inimical to life as we know it' (line 33).

m) What matter (other than meteors or meteorites) might hit the Earth from within or outside our Solar System?

n) What makes the writer suggest that the Earth might (still) be hit by a large comet or asteroid?

o) In one paragraph of 50–100 words, summarise what the passage says about the different extraterrestrial objects which do or which might collide with the Earth.

Exam Three

PAPER 4: LISTENING COMPREHENSION

Time: approx. 30 minutes

First part

For each of the questions 1–5, put a tick (√) in one of the boxes A, B, C or D, according to what you hear.

1. Which is the most accurate description of the condition of the trolley when it arrived?
   - A It was slashed, scratched and dented.
   - B It was scratched and dented in several places.
   - C It was dented all over and badly scratched.
   - D It had a number of scratches and one dent.

2. What would have appeared on the woman's order form?
   - A Mrs Y. Marsham TR6565 - 2.
   - B Mrs I. Marcham TR6655/2
   - C Mrs Y. Marchame TR6565/2
   - D Mrs U. Marshame TR6556 2

3. Who does the man in the Accounts Department really blame for the condition of the trolley?
   - A Nobody.
   - B The telephonist.
   - C The Post Office.
   - D The Customer Services Department.

4. How does the woman respond to the girl's comments about the complaints they get?
   - A With anger.
   - B With a compliment.
   - C With sarcasm.
   - D With understanding.

5. Why does the woman explain 'scratches' to the girl?
   - A She is trying to be helpful.
   - B She is showing her impatience.
   - C She doesn't want any more mistakes.
   - D She wants the nature of the damage to be fully understood.

Second part

For each of the questions 6–11, put a tick (√) in one of the boxes A, B, C or D, according to what you hear.

6. How is World Care sponsorship different from the other kinds mentioned?
   - A It has nothing to do with sport.
   - B It is a form of charity.
   - C It is voluntary.
   - D It is organised by the private citizen.

7 How much are you being asked to donate a month?
   A £8.50p.
   B Just under £250.
   C Roughly £85.
   D As much as you can afford.

8 What is an accurate description of the family he gives as an example?
   A A number of orphans.
   B A single-parent family with a number of children.
   C A mother and two children.
   D A poverty-stricken family, father on a low salary.

9 How does he say your own children will benefit?
   A They will be helped financially.
   B It will help them increase their knowledge of the world.
   C They will be given a sense of fulfilment.
   D They will appreciate things like television more.

10 What point does he emphasize about the scheme?
   A Children in both town and country are helped.
   B The child is always seen as a member of the community.
   C The children are from only the very poorest countries.
   D Each case is given individual attention.

11 What does he say will happen unless urgent action is taken?
   A Costs will rise.
   B Many will despair.
   C The problem will spread.
   D Many will die.

Third part

For questions 12 to 19, tick (√) whether these statements about the young man who is interviewed are true or false.

	True	False
12 He shares the interviewer's opinion of footballers' intellect.		
13 He represented England at football as a teenager.		
14 He spent his early childhood in South Africa.		
15 He left his country of origin in something of a hurry.		
16 He has returned to his native country during the past ten years.		
17 He would like to be seen as a leader of the anti-apartheid movement.		
18 He is sometimes insulted by fans at matches.		
19 He sincerely believes he will play in the country of his birth in the near future.		

Fourth part

For each of the questions 20–27 write all the answers given by the teams in the radio quiz and the correct answer given by the compère if neither team supplies it.

	Balsover Fliers Answer given (if any)	**Malvern Mounties** Answer given (if any)	Compère's Correct Answer (if not given)
	ROUND THREE		
20			
21			
22			
23			
	ROUND FOUR		
24			
25			
26			
27			

PAPER 5: INTERVIEW

Time: approx. 15 minutes

1 *Study this photo carefully, then describe it and be prepared to discuss one or more of the related topics (Note: In the Cambridge Proficiency Exam Interview, you will only see the photo; you will **not** see any instructions or discussion topics.)*

Describe:
- the people and their dress.
- the scene.
- the activity.

Discuss one of these:
- cruelty to animals.
- national dishes.
- vegetarianism.
- places in the world you would like to visit.

2 *Study one of these passages for a few moments. Then say **a)** where you think it might have come from, and **b)** who might have said or written it (to whom and when). Finally, what is your reaction to the passage?*

i) In the summer of 1982, 5,000 people turned out for a demonstration against the animal experimentation going on at the government's chemical warfare research centre at Porton Down. Several got inside the grounds, led by the new wave of anti-vivisectionists who run the British Union for the Abolition of Vivisection (BUAV). These are the 'hard' campaigners who have cut a swathe through the three or four bodies which have command of the funds and the loyalties of the 19th-century animal campaign bodies.

ii) It was a beautiful place for a holiday – you know, always hot and sunny, but not too oppressive. The only thing we couldn't get on with was the food. We've both travelled a lot and eaten some strange things, but there was something about the way they cooked most of their dishes that made us ill. In fact, after a few days all we really ate was masses and masses of fresh fruit – and some cereals which we'd taken with us.

3 *This is an advertisement published by the Research Defence Society in 1985. Study it carefully, and then be prepared to discuss the topics and questions below.*

Would you agree that this is a slightly unusual advertisement? Why/Why not? (What is it aiming to do?)
What's your own feeling about using animals for experiments and medical research?
Would you say many people in your own country would agree with you?

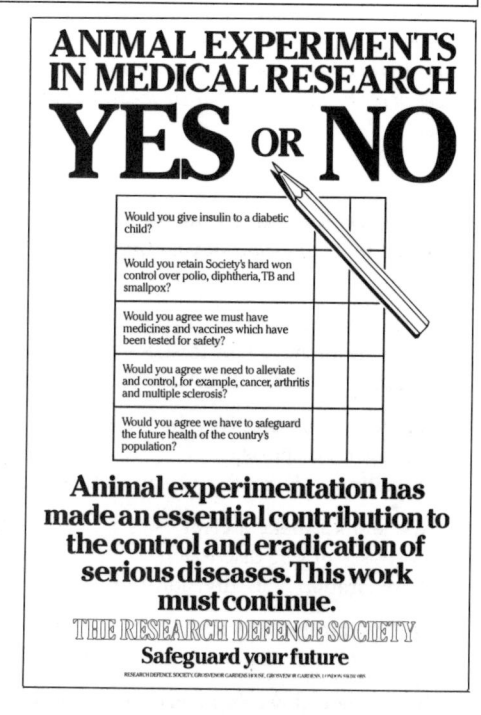

ANIMAL EXPERIMENTS IN MEDICAL RESEARCH
YES OR NO

- Would you give insulin to a diabetic child?
- Would you retain Society's hard won control over polio, diphtheria, TB and smallpox?
- Would you agree we must have medicines and vaccines which have been tested for safety?
- Would you agree we need to alleviate and control, for example, cancer, arthritis and multiple sclerosis?
- Would you agree we have to safeguard the future health of the country's population?

Animal experimentation has made an essential contribution to the control and eradication of serious diseases. This work must continue.

THE RESEARCH DEFENCE SOCIETY
Safeguard your future

(Exam One, Paper 5: Interview)

4 *Work in pairs. While you read this, your partner will read another report on page 18. Read this report and then tell your partner about it in your own words. Tell him or her what you think about the implications of the report and ask for his or her comments.*

Pickets help elderly

Picketing miners came to the help of 30 elderly ladies when the coach they were travelling in yesterday broke down near the Northport Colliery.

The ladies were returning from a half-day coach trip to the nearby city of Yorkbury. They had spent the afternoon visiting the cathedral and the old shopping centre. They were well over halfway home when the coach broke down.

Mr Stan Knight, the coach driver, said:

'The pickets were marvellous. I was driving along and suddenly the engine just cut out. I pulled the coach up just outside the colliery gates where there were about 15 pickets. As soon as they knew what the problem was, they rallied round and drove the ladies home in a number of cars.'

An hour later, Mr Knight was himself on his way home, thanks to the AA who came out to repair the engine.

Exam Four

PAPER 1: READING COMPREHENSION

Time: 1 hour

This paper is in two parts, Section A and Section B. For each question you answer correctly in Section A you gain one *mark; for each question you answer correctly in Section B you gain* two *marks. No marks are deducted for wrong answers. Answer all the questions. Indicate your choice of answer in every case on a separate sheet. Follow carefully the instructions about how to record your answer.*

Section A

In this Section you must choose the word or phrase which best completes each sentence. For each question, 1 to 25, indicate on your answer sheet the letter A, B, C or D against the number of the question.

1. This young author has already received the sort of . . . . that many older and wiser heads have had to strive a lifetime for.
   A attentiveness   B note   C recognition   D notoriety

2. There will of necessity be a . . . . to the amount of money put at the new manager's disposal.
   A ceiling   B roof   C sky   D summit

3. We should make a clear . . . . between 'competent' and 'proficient' for the purposes of our discussion.
   A separation   B division   C distinction   D difference

4. The young lad was the . . . . of his father.
   A image   B likeness   C picture   D portrait

5. They stood glowering at each other, eyeball to eyeball, their fists . . . . ready for action.
   A joined   B clenched   C clasped   D grasped

6. One wonders whether the current political . . . . is right for such a move.
   A environment   B climate   C state   D standpoint

7. The group's image . . . . to young people in general and the less well-off in particular.
   A appeals   B attracts   C excites   D draws

8. In . . . . , I must acknowledge that we were guilty of errors of judgement.
   A hindsight   B review   C experience   D retrospect

9. The supervisor's job is to . . . . the work of his particular department.
   A overlook   B overrun   C oversee   D overview

10. The employee's departure was hastened when he was caught with his hands in the . . . .
    A register   B accounts   C books   D till

11. In the unlikely . . . . of the film not being a box-office success, the producers stand to lose up to $15 million.
    A event   B happening   C eventuality   D incidence

12 She had never contemplated such a present, even in her . . . . dreams.
    A maddest   B commonest   C fieriest   D wildest

13 It is a sign of the times when a pop record can . . . . more money for charity than thousands of street and door-to-door collections.
    A fetch   B raise   C bring up   D subscribe

14 Rumours would suggest that the Board has one more ace up its . . . .
    A mind   B trouser-leg   C planning   D sleeve

15 The caddy trudged on round the . . . . , the bag of clubs over his shoulder feeling heavier at every hole.
    A court   B track   C rink   D course

16 In fact the criminal was . . . . from the country before extradition proceedings could be started.
    A interned   B exported   C deported   D barred

17 It tends to . . . . whenever I take my foot off the clutch, whether I'm in gear or not.
    A stumble   B pause   C stall   D crawl

18 Unless there is a . . . . in the next twenty-four hours, most of the weekend football matches are likely to be cancelled.
    A thaw   B freeze-up   C melt   D frost

19 Making mistakes is all . . . . of growing up.
    A chalk and cheese   B top and bottom   C part and parcel   D odds and ends

20 Despite scares to the contrary, we found that the elderly widow was . . . . all right.
    A perfectly   B anything but   C entirely   D far from

21 They agreed to call off the strike on . . . . that all those who had been dismissed were reinstated.
    A terms   B demand   C request   D condition

22 I wonder whether the lecturer will be up to the . . . . questions such an audience is capable of.
    A piercing   B examining   C searching   D cutting

23 It took us only a few hours to . . . . the paper off all four walls.
    A paste   B stroke   C scrape   D chip

24 There is . . . . to be a fortune on the sea-bed nearby.
    A rumoured   B whispered   C told   D written

25 The possibility of our suffering a major defeat cannot be . . . . out.
    A rubbed   B erased   C taken   D ruled

Section B

In this Section you will find after each of the passages a number of questions or unfinished statements about the passage, each with four suggested answers or ways of finishing. You must choose the one which you think fits best. For each question, 26 to 40, indicate **on your answer sheet** *the letter A, B, C or D against the number of the question. Give* **one answer only** *to each question. Read each passage right through before choosing your answers.*

First passage

FIRST the hamburger connection; now the songbird connection. The first link goes like this. Citizens of the United States are hungry for beef, especially in the form of fast foods such as hamburgers, frankfurters and the like. Yet beef has been one of the most inflationary items in the consumer's weekly shopping basket.

So the US government has authorised imports of so-called cheap beef from central America – beef raised on pasturelands established almost entirely at the cost of tropical forests. By trying to trim a nickel off the price of a hamburger, the US has contributed, albeit unwittingly but effectively and increasingly, to the massive loss of forests from southern Mexico to Panama.

Now the second link. A vast throng of North American songbirds spend their winters in Central America and the Caribbean – about two thirds of all woodland and forest species, totalling around half of all land birds breeding in North America. They include kingbirds, warblers, vireos, tanagers and peewees; more than 150 species altogether.

If you look around you on a warm winter's day in Belize or the Bahamas, every second bird you see is likely to hail from North America.

But the migrants have been running into trouble, according to Dr Eugene S. Morton and his colleagues at the Smithsonian Institution in Washington DC. When several billion birds leave North America each autumn, they find, on arriving in their wintering grounds of central America and the Caribbean, that their forest habitats have been succumbing to the machete and the match.

More than three-fifths of the forests have disappeared during the past 30 years, and at present rates of destruction, there will be virtually nothing left by the mid-1990s. Moreover, the adverse impact on migrant birds of this forest destruction is amplified several times over.

Because one acre of tropical forest may supply winter habitat to birds from 5 to 10 times as large an area in North America (due, among other reasons, to the disparate sizes of the two regions), the clearing of a patch of forest in, say, Mexico is equivalent to clearing many times as much forest in the north eastern United States.

So fewer birds are heading back each spring north of the border. Smithsonian scientists notice that species numbers are declining at rates between one and four per cent a year. The prospect is that there will be major reductions in throngs of forest-dwelling migrants. According to Professor John Terborgh of Princeton University, "We are, in effect, about to play observers in a massive experiment in which there will be dramatic alterations in the relative population sizes of numerous common species."

Ironically, it is precisely at the time of the songbirds' return that a number of insect species are likewise putting in a reappearance in North America. They tend to be at key phases of their life cycles, as larvae, etc., which leave them unusually vulnerable to insect-eating birds. The Smithsonian scientists speculate that the insect populations have thus far been held below levels at which they prove harmful to agricultural crops, through the predation pressures of huge numbers of songbirds returning over the horizon at just about the right time. If, however, the songbirds continue to decline, the insects could, within the foreseeable future, start to enjoy a population explosion every spring – which could mean bad news for US farmers.

26 According to the article, the US government has recently
  A arranged for forest land in Central America to be cleared.
  B seen a massive fall in the consumption of hamburgers.
  C bought up grazing land for cattle in Central America.
  D made it easier for Americans to buy meat at reduced prices.

27 The article suggests that
  A about 50% of winter birds around the Caribbean are from North America.
  B half the forests in Central America have been destroyed in the past three decades.
  C a third of all North American woodland birds migrate to Central America or the Caribbean.
  D very little forest land in the United States is inhabited by birds.

28 'Succumbing to the machete and the match' is a metaphor for:
  A being returned to a balanced ecology.
  B losing their fight against time.
  C being cut down and burnt.
  D being ploughed into the ground.

29 Why are the numbers of birds returning north declining annually?
  A There are fewer forests in the US for them to return to.
  B A huge experiment is being conducted on bird populations.
  C Tropical forests can support greater numbers now.
  D Their southern habitat is being drastically reduced.

30 The bad news for farmers in spring might be an increase in
  A the number of songbirds.
  B the number of insects.
  C the size of larvae.
  D the price of beef.

Second passage

DOES using a word processor affect a writer's style? The medium usually does do something to the message after all, even if Marshall McLuhan's claim that the medium simply is the message has been heard and largely forgotten now. The question matters. Ray Hammond, in his excellent guide *The Writer and the Word Processor* (Coronet £2.95 pp224), predicts that over half of the professional writers in Britain and the USA will be using word processors by the end of 1985. The best-known recruit is Len Deighton, from as long ago as 1968, though most users have only started since the micro-computer boom began in 1980.

Ironically word processing is in some ways psychologically more like writing in rough than typing, since it restores fluidity and provisionality to the text. The typist's dread of having to get out the Tippex, the scissors and paste, or of redoing the whole thing if he has any substantial second thoughts, can make him consistently choose the safer option in his sentences, or let something stand which he knows to be unsatisfactory or incomplete, out of weariness. In word processing the text is loosened up whilst still retaining the advantage of looking formally finished.

This has, I think, two apparently contradictory effects. The initial writing can become excessively sloppy and careless, in the expectation that it will be corrected later. That crucial first inspiration is never easy to recapture though, and therefore, on the other hand, the writing can become over-deliberated, lacking in flow and spontaneity, since revision becomes a larger part of composition. However these are faults easier to detect in others than in oneself. My own experience of the sheer difficulty of committing any words at all to the page means I'm grateful for all the help I can get.

For most writers, word processing quite rapidly comes to feel like the ideal method (and can always be a second step after drafting on paper if you prefer). Most of the writers interviewed by Hammond say it has improved their style ("immensely", says Deighton). Seeing your own words on a screen helps you to feel cool and detached about them.

Thus it is not just by freeing you from the labour of mechanical re-typing that a word processor can help you to write. One author (Terence Feely) claims it has increased his output by 400%. Possibly the feeling of having a reactive machine, which appears to do things, rather than just have things done with it, accounts for this – your slave works hard and so do you.

Are there no drawbacks? It costs a lot and takes time to learn – "expect to lose *weeks of work*", says Hammond, though days might be nearer the mark. Notoriously it is possible to lose work altogether on a word processor, and this happens to everybody at least once. The awareness that what you have written no longer exists at all anywhere, is unbelievably enraging and baffling.

Will word processing generally raise the level of professional writing then? Does it make writers better as well as more productive? Though all users insist it has done so for them individually, this is hard to believe. But reliance happens fast.

31 What appears to be changing rapidly in Britain and the USA?
   A The style writers are employing.
   B The medium authors are using.
   C The way new writers are being recruited.
   D The message authors are putting forward.

32 Typing a manuscript in the conventional manner may make a writer
   A take fewer risks.
   B make more mistakes.
   C become overcritical of his or her work.
   D have a lot of second thoughts.

33 One effect of using a word processor may be that the ongoing revision of a text
   A is done with too little attention.
   B produces a sloppy effect.
   C fails to produce a fluent style.
   D does not encourage one to pick up mistakes.

34 It is claimed here that word processors create
   A a feeling of distance between a writer and his or her work.
   B the illusion that you are the servant of the machine.
   C a sensation of power.
   D a reluctance in the author to express him- or herself.

35 As far as learning to use a word processor is concerned, the author of the passage feels that Hammond
   A is understating the problem.
   B exaggerates one drawback.
   C is too sceptical about the advantages.
   D overestimates the danger of losing text.

Third passage

Extract 1

Anita Brookner describes unhappiness and loneliness with unsettling skill. She takes us into the strange hotel looking over Lake Geneva and reminds us of other curious, lost hotels where people live in dreams and falsehoods, of the Hotel California and D.M. Thomas's White Hotel in particular. Her heroine is her best to date: withdrawn, precise, having an affair with a married man but remaining one of the observers of life who admire those with confidence. Her advantage over Anita Brookner's other heroines for me is that she has more sense of humour. The characters she half-envies she also half-despises. She describes their foibles with great wit. Indeed, I was left in no doubt as to who, of all the characters, is the most enviable – Edith Hope, who has a firm hold upon her own complicated identity.

Extract 2

One of the nicest presents I had for my birthday was a copy of *Hotel du Lac*. It's by Anita Brookner – you know, the woman who won the Booker Prize last year. I enjoyed reading it very much, and I think you would, too. It's just your kind of book. It's about a woman novelist who goes to stay in a hotel in Switzerland and – but I won't spoil it for you. I'll send it to you, if you like. Or perhaps you could try and get a copy from your local library – although I suspect there might well be a long waiting-list for it! I know it's very popular.

Extract 3

Anita Brookner, who is an international authority on eighteenth- and nineteenth-century painting, teaches at the Courtauld Institute of Art. In 1968 she was Slade Professor at Cambridge, the first woman ever to hold this position. She is the author of *Watteau, The Genius of the Future; Greuze; Jacques-Louis David;* and three other novels, *A Start in Life, Providence* and *Look at Me.*

With characteristic wit and beautifully observed detail, Anita Brookner has created perhaps her most memorable heroine yet. Edith Hope, as reluctant to be recruited by the ultra-feminine as by feminists, adept as a romantic writer yet contending with her own puzzled view of romance, comes marvellously to life in this humorous and touching new novel.

36 In all three extracts, *Hotel du Lac* is
    A commended for its wit and humour.
    B strongly recommended.
    C said to have a rather interesting heroine.
    D described as very popular.

37 Our impression of Edith Hope is of
    A a jealous, sensuous woman.
    B an ardent and passionate feminist.
    C a simple, romantic lady.
    D a complex and self-contradictory character.

38 What do extracts 1 and 3 both do?
    A Give an outline of the plot.
    B Make much of the leading character's personality.
    C Make mention of the heroine's sense of humour.
    D Compare *Hotel du Lac* with other novels.

39 Which of these statements is true?
    A Extract 1 gives the most objective information about the author.
    B Extract 2 expresses the most subjective reaction to the book.
    C Extract 3 tells us most about the setting for the novel.
    D All extracts employ a fairly formal tone.

40 Which of the three extracts could be from the back-cover information about the novel?
    A Extract 1.
    B Extract 2.
    C Extract 3.
    D None of them.

PAPER 2: COMPOSITION

Time: 2 hours

Write **two only** *of the following composition exercises. Your answers must follow exactly the instructions given. Write in pen, not pencil. You are allowed to make alterations, but see that your work is clear and easy to read.*

1 Suggest some ways in which the lives of the disabled and the elderly could be improved or made easier in your country. (About 350 words)

2 What do you think the world will be like in the year 2,000? Write a description of the way people lived as if for a history book in the year 2,100. (About 350 words)

3 Write, as if for a popular magazine, a short article entitled 'Impressions of a Disastrous Holiday'. (About 300 words)

4 This is part of an article which appeared in the local press:

> ### Hightown airport to expand
> Plans were announced by the Airport Authority yesterday to expand Hightown Airport.
>
> Since it was closed down as an RAF base shortly after the end of World War II, the airport has been the home of the Hightown Flying Club, with only occasional visits by larger aircraft.
>
> The Airport Authority now wish to improve the facilities in order to expand the airport to take commercial jet flights, including 747s. At an initial cost of £20 million, the Authority are hoping it will take some of the increasing air traffic now using Gatrow.

As a resident living near Hightown Airport, you are strongly opposed to its expansion – although you can see the need for another airport to take some of the load from Gatrow Airport. Write, in about 300 words, a reasoned letter of protest to the Director of the Airport Authority, stating your objections to the proposal.

5 *(This will be a choice of questions on the prescribed texts.)*

PAPER 3: USE OF ENGLISH

Time: 2 hours

Section A

1 *Fill each of the numbered blanks in the following passage with* **one** *suitable word.*

Rarely, if ever, ... (1) so much concern been expressed about our daily environment .... (2) at the present time. And oddly .... (3), ... (4) from those problems of heavy traffic, racial integration, overcrowding, and increasing crime and violence generally .... (5) with urban life, the concerns expressed in both town and country are very similar. True, many country villages .... (6) suffer .... (7) an increase in through-traffic, and crime is .... (8) the increase in rural areas, ... (9) probably at a slower rate .... (10) in towns and cities. But it is problems such as pollution, unemployment, human rights, energy and conservation which concern us .... (11), not just those who live in urban areas.

Even in Britain, ... (12) the majority of immigrants still live in cities, the challenge of the Multicultural Society will .... (13) reach rural areas in .... (14) village communities have remained virtually unchanged .... (15) hundreds of years. Such communities have already been touched (or tainted?) .... (16) pollution, unemployment and so on: they are .... (17) to face up to what to do with their young people, now that farming has become .... (18) mechanised, and to fight to conserve the countryside .... (19) the face of increasing industrialisation. What will be the consequences, one .... (20), when this rural population becomes multiracial?

2 *Finish each of the following sentences in such a way that it means exactly the same as the sentence printed before it.*

Example: They're processing my application now.
Answer: My application *is being processed now.*

a) 'You should have waited for us,' the team leader said to John.
The team leader criticised ....

b) It's possible that he didn't get my letter.
He might ....

c) The last time it snowed here was six years ago.
It ....

d) I only realised what I had I missed when they told me about it later.
Only when ....

e) There weren't nearly as many people there as I had expected.
There were far ....

f) When the Minister was asked about the strike, he declined to comment.
On ....

g) There was no need for you to have gone to all that trouble.
You ....

h) Please don't say things like that.
I wish ....

3 *Fill each of the blanks with a suitable word or phrase.*

Example: 'Would you like a coffee?'
'That's kind, but I'd *rather have* a cup of tea, if you don't mind.'

a) Her father . . . . 90 years old this week if he had lived.

b) I can't stand the way he's . . . . us what to do!

c) You . . . . to the concert with us last night. You would have enjoyed it.

d) '. . . . . so much to go sailing again for ages.'
'Well, why didn't you say so? We'll go tomorrow.'

e) You are . . . . on organising such a successful sales conference.

f) He's thought . . . . in 1900, but he's never told anyone exactly how old he is.

4 *For each of the sentences below, write a new sentence as similar as possible in meaning to the original sentence, but using the words given: these words* **must not be altered** *in any way.*

Example: I suggest you see a doctor as soon as possible.
advice
Answer: My advice (to you) is to see a doctor as soon as possible.

a) I'd like you to wait until they bring out a new model.
rather
....

b) We couldn't find the cat anywhere.
nowhere
....

c) What finally ended the dispute was the fact that the union agreed to go to arbitration.
agreement
....

d) He won't let anyone else touch his records.
objects
....

e) The fact that nobody said anything at the time surprised me.
what
....

f) The referee first blew the whistle 30 minutes into the game.
playing
....

g) I admitted it was my fault for burning the toast.
blame
....

h) It's becoming extremely expensive to maintain the museum.
upkeep
....

Section B

5 *Read the following passage, then answer the questions which follow it.*

Keeping your ideas to yourself

So you've got an invention – you and around 39,000 others each year, according to 1982 statistics!

The 64,000-dollar question, if you have come up with a device which you believe to be the answer to the energy crisis or you've invented a lawnmower which cuts grass with a jet of water (not so daft, someone has invented one), is how to ensure *you're* the one to reap the rewards of your ingenuity. How will all you garden shed boffins out there keep others from capitalising on your ideas and lining their pockets at your expense?

One of the first steps to protect your interests is to patent your invention. That can keep it out of the grasp of the pirates for at least the next 20 years. And for this reason inventors in their droves beat a constant trail from all over the country to the doors of an anonymous grey-fronted building just behind London's Holborn to try and patent their devices.

The building houses the Patent Office. It's an ant heap of corridors, offices and filing rooms – a sorting house and storage depot for one of the world's biggest and most varied collections of technical data. Some ten million patents – English and foreign – are listed there.

File after file, catalogue after catalogue detail the brain-children of inventors down the centuries, from a 1600's machine gun designed to fire square bullets at infidels and round ones at Christians, to present-day laser, nuclear and computer technology.

The first 'letters patent' were granted as long ago as 1449 to a Flemish craftsman by the name of John Utynam. The letters, written in Latin, are still on file at the office. They were granted by King Henry VI and entitled Utynam to 'import into this country' his knowledge of making stained glass windows in order to install such windows at Eton College.

Present-day patents procedure is a more sophisticated affair than getting a go-ahead note from the monarch. These days the strict procedures governing whether you get a patent for your revolutionary mouse-trap or solar-powered back-scratcher have been reduced to a pretty exact science.

From start to finish it will take around two and a half years and cost £165 for the inventor to gain patent protection for his brainchild. That's if he's lucky. By no means all who apply to the Patent Office, which is a branch of the Department of Trade, get a patent.

A key man at the Patent Office is Bernard Partridge, Principal Examiner (Administration), who boils down to one word the vital ingredient any inventor needs before he can hope to overcome the many hurdles in the complex procedure of obtaining a patent – 'ingenuity'.

'He's got to be ingenious', says Partridge. 'His invention must show a degree of inventiveness and ingenuity which another person aiming to produce an article to do the same task would not regard as the obvious answer to the problem.'

a) Why does the writer quote the example of a lawnmower which cuts grass with a jet of water?

b) Explain the phrase 'garden shed boffins' (line 12).

c) Why should anyone want to take out a patent?

d) Explain the phrase 'in their droves' (line 19).

e) Why couldn't the Patent Office be described as one of London's landmarks?

f) Why does the writer describe the Patent Office as 'an ant heap' (line 26)?

g) Explain in your own words the phrase 'the brain-children of inventors' (line 33).

h) Why are the 1600's machine gun and the present-day laser mentioned in the same sentence?

i) Why is John Utynam remembered?

j) Explain the phrase 'a more sophisticated affair' (lines 48–49).

k) How easy or difficult is it to obtain a patent for an invention?

l) Explain the phrase 'boils down to one word' (lines 65–66).

m) What characteristic must a good invention display before it will be granted a patent?

n) Summarise in 50–100 words what the passage says about the problems facing an inventor who wishes to patent an invention.

PAPER 4: LISTENING COMPREHENSION

Time: approx. 30 minutes

First part

For questions 1–10 tick (√) whether the statements are true or false.

		True	False	
1	A boy was recently drowned nearby.			1
2	Most of the island is a nature reserve.			2
3	The island is almost a perfect oval in shape.			3
4	There are very few buildings on the island.			4
5	The guide mentions the bird and reptile life on the island.			5
6	The guided tour of the island is optional.			6
7	This is the last stop on their day trip.			7
8	The ferry makes a number of short journeys each day.			8
9	When the youth says 'typical', he is criticising the guide.			9
10	There is some public disapproval of plans regarding a neighbouring island.			10

Second part

For questions 11, 12 and 13, put a tick (√) in one of the boxes, A, B, C or D.

11 What has the speaker been talking about up to now?
    A How to protect antiques from breakages.
    B Removing stains from furniture.
    C How to mend broken antiques of all kinds.
    D Valuing all kinds of antiques.

12 Why does the speaker mention a Persian rug?
    A As an example of a textile.
    B Because he's standing on one.
    C To compare it with a carpet.
    D Because someone has just shown him one with a bad stain on it.

13 According to the speaker, the removal of stains
    A nearly always takes days of hard work.
    B often requires a lot of patience.
    C always involves a weak solution of bleach.
    D should never be done with distilled water.

Third part

For questions 14–18, fill in the missing information. (The order of the 'Solutions' does not follow the points in the talk.)

To remove	Solution
14	Pour hot water through the material. Or use a weak solution of borax for dried stains.
15	Loosen with egg white, remove, then wash with warm soapy water. Alternatively, chill with ice and pick off.
16	Blotting or brown paper either side and apply hot iron. Then use white spirit.
17	Wash with warm soapy water. (Or add borax.) Alternatively, use white spirit.
18	Rub area with white spirit.

Fourth part

For questions 19 – 23, put a tick (√) in one of the boxes A, B, C or D, according to what you hear.

19 What is likely to have been the question put to the panel?
   A Do you welcome US influence on our everyday life?
   B Don't you think we are too dependent economically and politically on the US?
   C What are the major differences between the British and American way of life?
   D Shouldn't we try for closer political links with the US?

20 Sheila blames America for
   A the unstable British economy.
   B its own poor economic performance.
   C lowering moral standards in Britain.
   D refusing to remain a major ally.

21 Lord Watkins accuses Sheila of
   A being unpatriotic.
   B still looking for ways to dominate other countries.
   C underestimating the value of freedom.
   D not facing the realities of international relations.

22 Sheila's party would like to
   A halt American acts of aggression by force.
   B impose restrictions on US imports into the UK.
   C reduce the number of US missiles in the UK.
   D stop American goods coming into Britain.

23 Which of the speakers is openly opposed to the present government?
   A Sheila.
   B Lord Watkins.
   C Both of them.
   D Neither of them.

Fifth part

For questions 24–28, put a tick (√) in one of the boxes, A, B, C or D, according to what you hear.

24 What are Ronald's feelings about his father's funeral?
   A He is upset at not having known about it.
   B He wishes he hadn't attended.
   C He feels guilty for not bothering to come.
   D He is indifferent towards it.

25 The birthday Bobby recalls illustrates that
   A Ronald had artistic talent even then.
   B their father had no time for tobacco.
   C Bobby always chose unsuitable presents.
   D Ronald was their father's favourite.

26 What do we learn of Bobby's old girlfriend, Julie?
   A She was considered too good for Bobby.
   B She was made to feel unwelcome in the house.
   C She was one of Kate's rivals.
   D She was treated like a daughter when she visited.

27 Kate accuses Bobby of
   A loving his father too much.
   B feeling sorry for himself.
   C being too ambitious.
   D making her feel unwelcome.

28 Bobby's comments towards the end of the scene show that he
   A resents how Ronald neglected their father.
   B admires his brother's success.
   C feels sympathy for Ronald's private life.
   D hates his brother's dishonesty.

PAPER 5: INTERVIEW

Time: approx. 15 minutes

1 *Study this photo carefully, then describe it and be prepared to discuss one or more of the related topics (Note: In the Cambridge Proficiency Exam Interview, you will only see the photo; you will **not** see any instructions or discussion topics.)*

Describe:
— the people.
— the scene.
— the activities.

Discuss one of these:
— the influence of television.
— the problems of cramped living conditions.
— the place of the media in education.

2 *Study one of these passages for a few moments. Then say **a)** where you think it might have come from, and **b)** who might have said or written it (to whom and when). Finally, what is your reaction to the passage?*

i) What worries me is that there doesn't seem to be any discipline in schools nowadays – not like in my day. If you were late for school, or answered a teacher back, or didn't do your work properly – anything like that – we were punished. And as for playing truant, we only ever tried that once, I can assure you. Pity they're not as strict now. From what I've heard, the children can do just about anything they like.

ii) TIME: YOU CAN'T STORE IT OR BANK IT – YOU CAN ONLY LOSE IT OR USE IT. WHY NOT USE IT ON ADULT EDUCATION?

All College Certificate Courses are unit-based allowing a large degree of personal choice in selecting options to arrive at an individually planned and satisfying course of study. The courses have been organised for the student seeking a demanding and rigorous course pitched midway between full-time professionally orientated courses and non-vocational recreational courses.

Reduced fees, or full waiving of the fees, are available to applicants whose circumstances satisfy the Authority regulations.

3 *Study the figures below concerning further education in Britain: then be prepared to discuss the questions that follow.*

1982–83

Students at University 308,000
(including 48,000 post-graduate students and 34,000 from overseas)
Students at Polytechnics and Colleges of Higher
and Further Education (full-time advanced) 247,000
(including 30,000 from overseas – 42% from the Commonwealth
and 70% from developing countries)
Students at Colleges of Further Education (non-advanced courses) 390,000
Students released by employers for Further Education (part-time) 500,000
Part-time students, vocational and non-vocational 2,600,000

Percentage gaining University degree according to class of origin (father's occupation)

Born	1	2	3	4	5	6
1913–31	15.0	7.4	3.8	3.0	1.3	0.9
1932–47	27.0	17.6	5.8	5.1	2.3	2.4

Key
1 professional, high managerial   4 self-employed
2 lower professional, managerial 5 skilled manual workers
3 white collar   6 semi-skilled and unskilled

Which of the first set of figures do you find interesting – if any?
How do you think they compare with the situation in your own country?
What opportunities are there for part-time study where you live?
What does the second set of figures tell you about Britain?
Do you imagine the figures would be very different for students born after 1947?

Tapescripts for Paper 4: Listening Comprehension

Exam One Paper 4

TUTOR: Practice Exam One. Paper 4: Listening Comprehension. To hear each part again, rewind to the beginning. Look at page 14. **First Part.** Look at questions 1 to 7. You're going to hear the Headmaster of a school welcoming a guest speaker who has come along to give a talk. But first read the statements 1 to 7.

Now listen and tick whether the statements are true or false. Ready?

HEADMASTER: Good evening. Hm, hm. Good evening. . . . Good evening, ladies and gentlemen. Hm. May I first say what a pleasure it is to see so many of you here this evening.

Since its inception some one hundred and twenty years ago, this school has produced, 'released' some would say, sent out into the world thousands of talented young men and women who went on to achieve great success in their chosen field. A great many have achieved a certain fame, a few, it is only fair to say, a certain notoriety. However, I think I can pretty safely say that no Old Boy . . . and of course nowadays we must add 'Old Girl', has, if you like, captured the imagination of the public in the way that our guest speaker tonight has done.

For the past twelve months he has had not one, not two, but three of his plays running to packed audiences in the West End of London, and you have to go back a long way to match that particular achievement. And another, I gather, is at present in rehearsal and is due to open at the Prince of Wales' in four months' time. No-one would now begrudge him a place in the top echelons of British dramatists. If I may remind you briefly of some of the reviews his latest success received: 'Wickedly irreverent; don't miss it!' said *The Standard*; 'Hilarious! Sidesplitting!' from *The Mail*; 'The tears were rolling down my cheeks!' That was from *The Express*. I could go on all night.

He has of course also found time in the past five years to write two novels, the first of which, 'Quantity Before Quality' was an out-and-out best-seller, the sequel to which was the winner of last year's Thomas Rushton prize. There does indeed seem to be no limit to his talents.

We remember him here as a fine all-rounder, a hard worker, keen sportsman, of whom, to my undying shame, when Head of the English Department, I once wrote: 'tends to be rather idiosyncratic', and on another occasion – I hope all is forgiven – 'needs to develop a clearer style'.

Ladies and gentlemen, we are very grateful that such a busy man has been able and willing to find the time to be with us this evening. Would you please welcome – or rather, welcome back – Mr Andrew Barnes.

TUTOR: Now listen again and check your answers.
That's the end of the first part of the test.

TUTOR: **Second part**. Look at the newspaper advertisement on page 14. You're going to hear a telephone conversation with an agent for Worldwide Travel. But first read the advertisement.

Now listen, and for questions 8 to 13, write corrections to the mistakes in the advertisement. Ready?

MAN: Worldwide Travel. Can I help you?

WOMAN: Yes, I'm ringing about your advertisement in last night's *Bugle*.

MAN: Yes? Er, which one, madam? We had two or three adverts in the paper yesterday evening.

WOMAN: Oh, the one about er a dozen places left on a holiday to Spain, next month.

MAN: Oh – that one!

WOMAN: Sorry?

MAN: Well, we've had a number of calls about that ad and it seems that between one of our secretaries and the printer, a number of er errors somehow er crept into it.

WOMAN: You mean there aren't a dozen places left on it?

MAN: No, I'm afraid there were only a couple of places left, not twelve, . . .

WOMAN: And I suppose they've been taken, have they?

MAN: Well actually no, not yet.

WOMAN: Really? The . . . the other details were right, were they? I mean, a fortnight's full board for £210?

MAN: Well no, I'm sorry to say it should have read *half* board for £410.

WOMAN: Are you telling me . . .?

MAN: Yes, I'm terribly sorry, madam. We have put a correction and, of course, an apology in for this evening, . . .

WOMAN: But that's not good enough, is it? . . . I really don't know what to say. I suppose my husband and I might just still be interested, especially if the accommodation is really a first-class hotel and we could go in April, which is when . . .

MAN: Well, er . . .

WOMAN: Don't tell me. We can't go in April.

MAN: That is unfortunately the case, madam. The offer is regrettably for March only. Another 'error', I'm afraid. And before you ask, the accommodation *is* first-class . . . no doubt about that, . . .

WOMAN: Oh, so you got something right, then.

MAN: . . . but it's not exactly a first-class hotel, if you see what I mean.

WOMAN: No.

MAN: Well, our clients will be housed in . . .

WOMAN: Oh don't bother. It's pretty obvious that your advertisement was totally misleading!

MAN: It wasn't meant to be, madam, I can assure you. If it hadn't been for the fact that . . .

WOMAN: I can understand now why it took me so long to get hold of you in the first place.

MAN: Ah yes, the . . . the number in the paper. Yes, I'm sorry about that. Can't think how it happened.

WOMAN: Well you might bear in mind in future that getting the last two digits of a telephone number the wrong way round can make life very frustrating for someone trying to make a call, . . .

MAN: Yes, my apologies, madam, . . .

WOMAN: Well, I'm sorry, but it's just not good enough. I shall most certainly be writing to the Advertising Standards . . .

TUTOR: Now listen again and check your answers.
That's the end of the second part of the test.

TUTOR: **Third part**. Look at questions 14 to 18 on page 15. You're going to hear an item of radio news. But first read the multiple-choice questions.

Now listen and put a tick in one of the boxes – A, B, C or D – for questions 14 to 18. Ready?

READER: There has been a bizarre new twist following the ugly scenes which took place early yesterday evening between supporters of Broadmoor Town and their rivals for promotion this year, Wormwood Rangers, following their afternoon match at the Broadmoor ground. Reports were coming in only late this morning of an incident in which some twenty Broadmoor supporters were trapped in a local café by a gang of Wormwood fans armed with stones, knives and assorted other weapons. The 'siege' is believed to have gone on for the best part of an hour before the police were alerted and the visiting team's fans were dispersed. The owner of the café, Mr Michael Watson, who has been running his East Side establishment for the past seventeen and a half years, said today that he would be selling up and closing down as soon as he possibly could. David Morgan reports.

MORGAN: And with me, in Church Street, just outside Mad Mike's café, is Michael Watson, who was unfortunate enough to be caught up yesterday in some of the worst scenes of soccer violence seen so

WATSON: far this season. Mr Watson, is it true that you've decided to shut down the café?
Yeh well, I reckon enough's enough. I been here for the best part of twenty years and... well, there's been... we've had our fair share of trouble in the past, but... nothing like this... nothing compared to what those animals did when...

MORGAN: Could you tell us exactly what did happen while...?

WATSON: Well, yeh, I was inside like, washing up, and I don't know, about twenty local lads came in after the match, about six, half past...

MORGAN: They were regular customers of yours, were they?

WATSON: Oh I wouldn't say that. I seen most of them before. Anyway, they ordered hamburgers all round, and they were sitting around, playing the fruit machines and the video games, you know, the normal sort of thing, when this gang of Wormwood supporters sort of burst in.

MORGAN: How do you know they were...?

WATSON: You could tell. They had scarves and rosettes and things. And well, the Broadmoor boys see didn't react, and then these others started turning over tables and chairs and... you know, the language! Then a few fights broke out and well, in the end the Wormwood lot left, but they just sort of hung about outside, shouting, making a hell of a din. And then, when the Broadmoor boys tried to leave, they just stopped them, pushed them back inside. And then things started coming through the windows; as you can see, there's hardly a pane of glass not broken. Stones, hammers, even a dustbin got thrown in.

READER: David Morgan spoke later to Superintendent Scott of the local constabulary.

SCOTT: Of course, inevitably, fingers are going to be pointed at us, and we're going to get the old calls for more policing at matches. Let me tell you, there were more police on duty at this match than we have ever had before at a League game. We could hardly have foreseen trouble such as that in the café you're talking about. We're not fortune-tellers, you know. Until we get stiffer sentences from the magistrates, we in the police are always going to be on the losing side.

READER: A spokesman for the Ministry of Sport said that they would be making a full statement after sifting through police reports. This and other similar incidents is a severe setback to the government's newly-launched campaign to clamp down on football hooliganism. Mr Byrne, the Minister for Sport, was already due to meet Football Association members a week on Tuesday.

TUTOR: Now listen again and check your answers.
That's the end of the third part of the test.

TUTOR: **Fourth part**. Look at questions 19 to 24 on page 16. You're going to hear the final extract of a short story read on the radio. But first read the six multiple-choice questions.

Now listen and put a tick in one of the boxes – A, B, C or D – for questions 19 to 24. Ready?

WOMAN: And now, Henry Whiting reads the last part of *Going Back* by N. A. Smart, adapted for radio by George Walker.

WHITING: I had just sat down and opened the menu. It was as if she had been expecting me, as if we had arranged to meet the night before. She came straight to my table, smiling, her arm outstretched. Within seconds, the waiter had brought aperitifs and we were talking wildly, questioning and answering, laughing between smiles. She had grown: larger, fuller, yes, even fatter. The 'princess' title I had bestowed upon her seemed much less apposite than before. And yet... I explained I had been to a conference in the town the day before. She smiled again; she had read about it in the local paper. She felt I had changed very little.

When we had finished eating and paid – she insisted on separate bills, as had always been her wont – we embarked on a stroll by the river. We passed the tree where nine years before we had knelt in the mud, naive and innocent, and carved our names. Had she forgotten? Had all that passed from her mind? She kicked the gravel path and laughed quietly. I thought as much. She had not forgotten. We walked on. As time passed, our bursts of conversation became shorter, less animated, and the pauses between them correspondingly longer. It was one of those cold November days when morning is followed by evening and the afternoon seems to be missed out completely. I told her that her English had improved. She grinned, for she knew it was much less fluent than it had been. And how had she been? She was right. I had already asked her. Three times. We finished the walk in silence. By the time we arrived at the square again, the sun had set and it was getting dark. I had mentally already bidden her farewell when she invited me back to her house. The old house? On the hill? No, they had sold that. Her mother had died. I was sorry. She poured two large cognacs and disappeared into the sitting room. I followed to find her sitting by the fire. I recalled how she had always liked the position; in the old house. It was only when I saw her with the firelight behind her that I realised how much she had changed. No, I hadn't written. No, I hadn't wanted to come back before. No, I hadn't expected to see her.

I was sure she was going to stretch her hand over the table towards me when something moved behind us. A little girl had come into the room, unnoticed. She had a face I had seen somewhere before that glowed with innocence. Very beautiful. She suddenly looked at me, as if she hadn't noticed me there earlier, then turned and, strangely without feeling, whispered something in the direction of the fire. Even my meagre smattering of Chinese enabled me to glean she was telling her mother that her father was waiting in the dining room.

TUTOR: Now listen again and check your answers.
And that's the end of the test for Exam One.

Exam Two Paper 4

TUTOR: Practice Exam Two. Paper 4: Listening Comprehension. To hear each part again, rewind to the beginning. Look at page 31. **First part**. Look at questions 1 to 5. You're going to hear a radio talk on one aspect of English. But first read the multiple-choice questions.

Now listen and put a tick in one of the boxes – A, B, C or D – for questions 1 to 5. Ready?

ANNOUNCER: And now for the fourth in our short series of talks about English. This week's talk is about eponyms. Marjory Small explains.

MARJORY: Eponyms are fascinating things. We all use words like 'biro', 'blanket', 'cardigan', 'hooligan', 'mackintosh', 'a Darby and Joan Club', 'a Gladstone bag', 'a nosey parker' – oh, I could go on for ever. English (and I suspect other languages, too, in their own way) is full of them. They're eponyms.

So what is an eponym? Quite simply, it's a word or phrase that's come into the language through a person's name or something a person was famous for. The word or expression derives from the name.

Wellington boots, often called *wellies* now, started life as high leather boots which covered the knee in front and were cut away at the back. They were named after Arthur Wellesley, the First Duke of Wellington (1769–1852) who was known as the Iron Duke. The fact that *wellies* are now waterproof rubber boots that reach to the knee is neither here nor there.

But let's go back to one or two of the words and expressions I quoted at the beginning. What about 'hooligan'? And 'hooliganism'? The *Longman Dictionary of Contemporary English* defines a hooligan as a 'noisy, rough person who causes trouble by fighting, breaking things, etc.' (I like the etcetera; it means you can imagine all sorts of things.) But it doesn't sound a very *English* word – at least, not to me. So where did it come from? A *Dictionary of Slang* (by Partridge) quotes as the source a book entitled *Hooligan Nights* written in 1899 by Clarence Rook. Rook maintains that there was a man called Patrick Hooligan who at about that time 'walked to and fro among his fellow men, robbing them and occasionally bashing them'. So that, apparently, is that.

I mentioned earlier the expression 'a nosey parker'. If someone is *nosey*, of course, he or she is interested in things that do not concern him or her. But why 'a nosey *parker*'? According to one book I referred to, the expression derives from a Dr Matthew Parker (1504–75), who was an Archbishop of Canterbury. I won't go into the details of his career, which was a somewhat chequered one, by all accounts, except to say that he was fanatically religious and acquired a reputation for scrutinising all matters of Church business. We can only assume therefore that anyone who pried too much and too often into other people's affairs came to be known after that as a 'nosey parker'.

And, finally, what about 'blanket'? It's surprising, isn't it, how many everyday household words are in fact eponyms. The origin of this particular word seems to be in some doubt, but one suggestion is that some of the first blankets produced in England were spun on the looms of a weaver called Blanket, who set up shop in Bristol around the middle of the fourteenth century. If that is the case, it's one of our older eponyms.

ANNOUNCER: If you'd like to look out for more, or write to us about the derivations of other such words, why don't you . . .?

TUTOR: Now listen again and check your answers.
That's the end of the first part of the test.

TUTOR: **Second part**. Look at questions 6 to 11 on page 32. You're going to hear one side of a telephone conversation between the receptionist of The Whitechapel Hotel and a prospective guest at the hotel. But first read the information on the hotel reservation sheet.

Now listen and fill in the reservation sheet for the new guest. Questions 6 to 11. Be careful; the information is not given in the same sequence as the questions. Ready?

RECEPTION: Whitechapel Hotel. Can I help you?
(*pause*)
Er yes, sir, we have. Would that be a single room or a double?
(*pause*)
I see. Well, it's £27.50 for both a double and a twin-bedded room, £35 with shower.
(*pause*)
You'd like a private shower; right, sir.
(*pause*)
Rather than a twin-bedded room. I see, sir.
(*pause*)
Yes, it does, sir. English or Continental. And also included in the quoted price is V.A.T. at 15%.
(*pause*)
Good. Did you say the weekend after next, sir?
(*pause*)
So that would be the nights of the 30th and the 31st, wouldn't it? I mean, May the 1st – I'm sorry, I'm dreaming.
(*pause*)
Yes, April madness! Could I have your name, sir?
(*pause*)
Is that G-I-L-E-S?
(*pause*)
Ah, Y not I, I'm sorry, sir.
(*pause*)
And could you give me your initials, please?
(*pause*)
V.J. Thank you. Er, is there a telephone number you can give, er a contact number, just in case we . . .
(*pause*)
Yes, I know; it's not something that many hotels do, but we like to have one – as I say, just in case . . .
(*pause*)
York, 4 0 double 6 8, I see. Er, do you happen to know the area code for York off hand?
(*pause*)
0 9 0 4. Thank you very much.

(*pause*)
No, no. It's just a precaution, I assure you. We very rarely need it.
(*pause*)
Well, we're a medium-sized hotel – not as big, I'm sure, as some of the ones you've got back home in The States, but er I'm sure you and your wife will be very happy here.
(*pause*)
Is there anything else . . .?

TUTOR: Now listen again and check your answers.
And that's the end of the second part of the test.

TUTOR: **Third part**. Look at the map on page 33. You're going to hear a continuation of the telephone conversation between Mr Gyles and the receptionist. But first study the list of places and look carefully at the map.

Now listen and write the numbers of the places in the appropriate boxes on the map. Three of the boxed places on the map are not mentioned.
Ready?

RECEPTION: Is there anything else I can tell you?
(*pause*)
Oh, yes, Mr Gyles, we certainly are. In fact we're mid-way between the main train station to the north and the coach station to the south, so we're easily accessible. Both are only a couple of minutes away by taxi.
(*pause*)
Oh no, the hotel was established at the turn of the century.
(*pause*)
Well yes, we're pretty ideally situated, very near the centre of things.
(*pause*)
Yes, there's one just round the corner from the hotel: they've got a season at the moment. Quite often they get pre-London productions there; in fact next week, while you're here, they're doing a new Tom Stoppard play which might interest you . . .
(*pause*)
Oh yes, just about opposite the hotel there's one – one of those that's split into three, so you get a good choice, and one of them has continuous performances all through the night. I'm afraid I can't tell you what they're showing next week off hand, but if you'd like to wait a . . .
(*pause*)
Oh, yes. In fact, from the bedrooms at the rear of the hotel you can see the old drawbridge and tower. And just on the other side of the castle, in fact, going away from the hotel, but still only about ten minutes' walk away, is one of the best collections of eighteenth-century paintings in the whole of the south. That's normally a must for the tourist.
(*pause*)
Not at all.
(*pause*)
Ha, yes, there is one, about three hundred metres along from the hotel, in the same street, in fact. You do normally have to be a member, but I know they do have an arrangement for er short-term visitors, so yes, I'm sure you would be welcomed there er if you're feeling lucky one of your evenings here.
(*pause*)
That's quite all right. We'll look forward to welcoming you here on the 30th.
(*pause*)
Goodbye, Mr Gyles.

TUTOR: Now listen again and check your answers.
And that's the end of the third part of the test.

TUTOR: **Fourth part**. Look at questions 19 to 27 on page 34. You're going to hear someone explaining a procedure to a friend. You must decide in which order, according to this person, those tools and other things will be used. But first have a good look at the pictures.

Now listen and write 1, 2, 3, 4 etc. in the box beside each picture, 1 for the first thing you need, 2 for the second, and so on. Ready?

DICK: I only want to know basically, you know, in layman's terms, what I've got to do.
TOM: Well, have you got a bit of paper? You won't be able to remember all of it.
DICK: O.K. Er, yes.
TOM: Right, first thing. Er, when you get the door, you'll probably find . . . I expect it'll have what they call horns on the top and the bottom – they usually do. I've

TOM: never discovered why they call them horns, but I think they're on the door to sort of give it some protection when it's being moved around. Anyway, they have to be sawn off before you can do anything. All right?

DICK: What, they're just blocks of wood, are they?

TOM: Yeh, just four little bits sticking out from top and bottom. O.K.? So then you've got to lay the door on its side, with the lock facing down, on the floor, . . .

DICK: Yeh.

TOM: . . . And er use a plane to trim the long edge, get it nice and flat.

DICK: You mean it doesn't arrive nice and smooth?

TOM: No, it's usually quite a rough edge, 'cause you've obviously got to get it down to exactly the right size for your er doorway, haven't you? This is what I mean, you see. It's not an easy job; it's really a job for an expert.

DICK: Well, let's go on, anyway.

TOM: Well, if you think you can do it. So you've planed down that edge, all right? Then you get a measure and measure the exact width you want, O.K.? Leaving about 3 millimetres for clearance on either side of the frame. Yes?

DICK: Yeh.

TOM: And you mark the door at the top and the bottom, then draw a line joining the two marks. Now then you've got to turn the door over on to the other side, so that the lock side is facing upwards now, you see what I mean, and then er plane that whole edge down to the line you've drawn. Got it?

DICK: Mm. Yeh.

TOM: Well, do roughly the same for the height of the door, but leaving er what is it? – about 3 millimetres at the top, I think it is, and about double, about 6 millimetres at the bottom. And you do the marking and the planing the same. Oh, I forgot. To get it er right, you know the door in the frame – to get your marks in the right place, you'll probably need to put the door on wedges, support it on thin, shallow wedges, or else you'll find it difficult to get it exactly the right size. I suppose you could use something else to prop it up on, if you can't find the proper things. Anyway, . . . you with me so far?

DICK: Yeh, I think so.

TOM: Well, then you need to stand the door on the wedges again, or whatever you're using – and stand it in the doorway, and . . . er mark very carefully on the door where you need the hinges to be. And you have to be extra-specially careful here, or you could ruin the whole thing in about thirty seconds flat.

DICK: All right.

TOM: So mark where the hinges are going to go, top and bottom; then get the two hinges and place them on the door, at the edge, where they're going to be on the door, you see? and trace round them carefully. And then er, you've got to chisel out a recess for them to go into; careful which side of the chisel you're using, O.K.? And then, drill little holes into the recesses you've chiselled out, usually three for each hinge, isn't it? Better with a manual drill, I find, that sort of job, rather than an electric one. Then screw the hinges on the door, and you're just about there. Get the door back on the wedges, screw the other flap of the hinges on to the frame – where the old hinges were – and with any luck it won't fall and hit you over the head.

DICK: Well thanks.

TOM: If on the other hand it does, don't say I didn't warn you.

TUTOR: Now listen again and check your answers.

And that's the end of the test for Exam Two.

Exam Three Paper 4

TUTOR:	Practice Exam Three. Paper 4: Listening Comprehension. To hear each part again, rewind to the beginning. Look at page 49. **First part**. Look at questions 1 to 5. You're going to hear a woman phoning a firm about a recent purchase. But first read the multiple-choice questions.
	Now listen and put a tick in one of the boxes – A, B, C or D – for questions 1 to 5. Ready?
RECEPTION:	First Class Mail Order. Can I help you?
WOMAN:	Yes, I'm ringing about a trolley I ordered from you.
RECEPTION:	Yes?
WOMAN:	Well, when it arrived, I found the packing had been slashed and the trolley was badly scratched . . .
RECEPTION:	Can I have . . . ?
WOMAN:	Down to the metalwork it was in places, and on the handle part it was actually dented in one place. Overall it was a complete mess.
RECEPTION:	I see. Er, . . . can you tell me when you ordered it, please?
WOMAN:	Yes, wait a moment. It's on my copy of the order here somewhere. Ah yes, I ordered it on . . . 13th March.
RECEPTION:	I see, madam. And er could I have your name, please?
WOMAN:	Yes. It's Mrs Marchame. Mrs Y. Marchame.
RECEPTION:	Is that er M-A-R-S-H-A-M?
WOMAN:	No, C-H-A-M, and an E at the end.
RECEPTION:	Oh. And can you give me the order number, please?
WOMAN:	Ah, well that's . . . er TR6565 stroke 2.
RECEPTION:	TR6565 stroke 2?
WOMAN:	Yes. It was a trolley with a red frame.
RECEPTION:	Yes. Well, I'll just put you through to someone who can help you.
WOMAN:	Well, thank you. . . . But I've just given you . . .
	(*pause*)
WOMAN:	Come on.
	(*pause*)
MAN:	Accounts. Can I help you?
WOMAN:	Well, I'm not sure I wanted to speak to anyone in Accounts.
MAN:	Oh. Oh, it's . . . new girl on the switchboard . . .
WOMAN:	You see, I was ringing about a trolley I ordered from you, and I gave all the infor . . .
MAN:	I see. And I suppose the trolley hasn't arrived yet. Is that it? Some industrial dispute at the post office, I supp . . .
WOMAN:	No, no, it's arrived all right.
MAN:	It has arrived? Well, why . . . ?
WOMAN:	Yes, but it's the condition it was in that I was ringing about.
MAN:	Oh, you want to make a complaint about a trolley that has arrived, but which was er . . .
WOMAN:	Well yes, . . . if it's not too much trouble.
MAN:	Oh I think I'm beginning to understand.
WOMAN:	Good.
MAN:	Look, I'll put you through to the Customer Services Department; that lot'll be able to sort you out.
WOMAN:	You're very kind.
MAN:	That's what we're here for.
WOMAN:	Who'd have guessed!
	(*pause*)
GIRL:	Hello, Customer Services.
WOMAN:	Hello, my name's Marchame . . . spelt with a C and an E at the end. You do deal with complaints, do you?
GIRL:	Well, that rather depends on the nature of the complaint.
WOMAN:	Oh that's nice.
GIRL:	Well, you see, Mrs Matcham, . . .
WOMAN:	Marchame!
GIRL:	Oh sorry. You see, we do receive a number of what you might call trivial complaints.
WOMAN:	Charming.
GIRL:	Of course I'm not suggesting that . . .
WOMAN:	No, well look, I haven't got all day. The thing is, I ordered a trolley – a red trolley – from you, it seems like about ten years ago at the moment. And when it arrived, it had scratches all over it.
GIRL:	Scratches?
WOMAN:	Yes, you know, those little marks you can make with your nails or a cat makes when . . .
GIRL:	Yes, I know what . . .
WOMAN:	Oh never mind. The packing had been cut to ribbons and the article had been quite clearly damaged as a result.
GIRL:	Well, I'm afraid in that case I'll have to put you through to the area manager, who . . .
WOMAN:	I don't believe it!
GIRL:	If you'd like to hold on, . . .

79

TUTOR: Now listen again and check your answers.
That's the end of the first part of the test.

TUTOR: **Second part**. Look at questions 6 to 11 on pages 49 and 50. You're going to hear a broadcast appeal. But first read the six multiple-choice questions.

Now listen and put a tick in one of the boxes – A, B, C or D – for questions 6 to 11. Ready?

ANNOUNCER: And now an appeal on behalf of the World Care Organisation by Richard Falcon.

RICHARD: Good evening. Tonight I want to talk to you about sponsorship. Sponsorship is all around us in the eighties, isn't it? Sporting events, trade fairs, voyages of discovery – where would they be without it? But I'm going to ask you to consider a rather different kind of sponsorship. For the best part of four decades, World Care has been organising sponsorship of children in poverty-stricken areas of the Third World. This child you see here on your screen is only in that classroom because of the efforts of our volunteer staff and the goodwill of his sponsor. It may be difficult to imagine that an eight-pound-fifty-a-month sponsorship can achieve anything so dramatic, but, believe me, it can. To a fatherless family in Southeast Asia surviving on under £250 a year, for instance, it makes a great deal possible. It makes health and education possible for a small son or daughter. A skill training possible for the widowed mother and more to eat for all the children. If you have children of your own, you can give them a much deeper and more rewarding experience with a 'friendship through sponsorship' than anything the TV can offer. Does your heart say 'yes' while your head says 'but'? But can our help really change anything? But is the money well spent? With 3,000 projects in 65 developing countries, with 35 years' experience, with some 400,000 children already being helped towards lives worth living, we think the answer is 'yes'. What matters more, though, is that we tackle the job one child at a time. Right there in the villages or in the slums, our people are daily turning your help into a solid reality. During those precious childhood years, your boy or girl is learning new skills and gaining confidence, the surrounding community is working towards self-reliance. One day these things will come together to create a real future . . . but it won't begin without your backing.

And time is of the essence. We must start equipping them with health, strength and confidence while they're still young – and before the crushing burden of hopelessness hits them. Once you can say 'yes', not only can we confirm your sponsorship and introduce you to your child through his or her picture folder, but we can transfer our costs of looking after your child to another needy child in another community. That's how, one at a time, the battle for poverty's children is being won. You see, we're asking for a hand up, not a hand-out. Join us now in the wonderfully satisfying work of putting smiles back on faces like these. If you have fought through to a better life, now help a child to do the same.

The address to write to: P.O. Box . . .

TUTOR: Now listen again and check your answers.
That's the end of the second part of the test.

TUTOR: **Third part**. Look at questions 12 to 19 on page 50. You're going to hear a short radio interview with a professional sportsman. But first read the questions.

Now listen and tick whether the statements 12 to 19 are true or false. Ready?

INTERVIEWER: I think it wouldn't be unfair to suggest, Terry, that, as an educated young man with seven O Levels and two A Levels – in History and French – you are something of an exception in a world in which er players are not famous for the shall we say . . . the power of their intellect.

TERRY: I'm not so sure that is fair, really, Brian. Perhaps thirty years ago it would have been, but in recent times you've had graduates playing international football for . . . England and Scotland . . . and Ireland. I think . . .

INTERVIEWER: True, but there must be some truth in that famous quote from a League club chairman, who said er . . . that most

	footballers haven't got what it takes to run a fish and chip shop. But apart from that, Terry, you are unique, or at least exceptional, in that you have succeeded here, not British by birth, black in what is still a white man's game, and from a background that... well, didn't promise that much, am I right?
TERRY:	Well, I don't know about not promising too much; it was hard, sure, but we didn't starve. But the rest, yes, I suppose I have to count myself very lucky er to have become an international player here so young and er...
INTERVIEWER:	Playing for England before your twentieth birthday, weren't you?
TERRY:	That's right.
INTERVIEWER:	Of course you're South African by birth, aren't you?
TERRY:	Yeh, I was born in Cape Town.
INTERVIEWER:	And stayed there until you were...?
TERRY:	Coming up ten. My father was sort of arrested – he was pretty active in the anti-apartheid movement – and he got put under house arrest. But as it happened, with the help of friends and so on, all eight of us, father, mother and brothers, we got our one-way ticket to London. A matter of some urgency, you might say.
INTERVIEWER:	And you haven't been back since.
TERRY:	Huh huh. I could if I wanted to now. I've got a British passport, but er the opportunity hasn't... or perhaps it's the motivation that's lacking.
INTERVIEWER:	And yet you do feel strongly about what is going on in South Africa, isn't that so?
TERRY:	I do, yes. Probably not as strongly as some of my family do, but yes, I have a lot of contacts with non-racial organisations in South Africa. You know, I guess because of my position, you know, because of the football, people seem to think I should be doing more, that I should stand on a soap-box and become a sort of spokesman for blacks in the old country. But I don't see myself as that sort of figure. Not my scene, if you like.
INTERVIEWER:	Do you feel the fans treat you differently from the rest of the team?
TERRY:	What, our own fans, or the opposing teams?
INTERVIEWER:	Both.
TERRY:	Oh, the other teams' supporters quite often give me a hard time, get on my back in a game, you know, chanting a bit of abuse. I mean, I'm quite a good target, aren't I? But it's the same for most black players; you'll always get a section of the crowd who enjoy having a go at us.
INTERVIEWER:	What memories do you have of Cape Town?
TERRY:	The football. Playing in the street. Often barefoot. As you said, we weren't that well-off.
INTERVIEWER:	We always associate South Africa with rugby. You didn't play rugby rather than football?
TERRY:	No. Rugby is very much the white man's sport in South Africa. Football is much more popular with the blacks and coloureds there.
INTERVIEWER:	And one final question, Terry. Er, can you envisage a day when you might go back as a player? Would you play there?
TERRY:	Not under the present regime, no. And I'd have thought it unlikely that it would change much in my playing career. I may be wrong, but... It's sad, but there it is.
INTERVIEWER:	Well, thank you, Terry. Nice to talk to you.
TERRY:	Thank you, Brian.
TUTOR:	Now listen again and check your answers. That's the end of the third part of the test.
TUTOR:	**Fourth part**. Look at questions 20 to 27 on page 51. You're going to hear part of a radio quiz on the early days of the motor car. The contest is between two veteran car clubs calling themselves the Balsover Fliers and the Malvern Mounties. But first look at the scorecard.
	Now listen and write down all the answers that are given by the teams and the correct answer if neither team supplies it. Ready?
COMPERE:	Right, straight into Round Three, which is all about years. To get your two points you have to be within two years of the correct answer. If you're not, the question goes over to the opposing team. So, question 20, for the Balsover Fliers: in which year was the Austin car company formed?
BILL:	Er... (WHISPERS)... Nineteen, er... Nineteen o six?
COMPERE:	That's near enough. In fact it was one year earlier, but that's good enough for your maximum points. Question 21, Malvern Mounties, in which year did

	Daimler and Benz merge to make the first Mercedes Benz?
MALCOLM:	Ooh, must be, well, between the wars.
COMPERE:	I need more than that.
MALCOLM:	Nineteen, nineteen thirty?
COMPERE:	No, I'm sorry. Over it goes. Anybody?
BOB:	Nineteen twenty six.
COMPERE:	Spot on. Your own question, Balsover, question 22: in which year was the self-starter introduced?
BOB:	Nineteen twelve? Nineteen eleven?
COMPERE:	Which one do you want?
BOB:	(WHISPERS) Nineteen eleven.
COMPERE:	Ha, first ideas are always the best. Still, two points.
BOB:	Twelve, was it? Oh.
COMPERE:	And finally for Malvern: when did Daimler produce his first car?
MERVYN:	Er, must have been around er 1896?
COMPERE:	Can't let you have that. Fliers?
BILL:	(WHISPERS) Just a guess. Er 1899?
COMPERE:	Oh no, going the wrong way. You were nearer, Malvern, but I'm afraid you were exactly a decade too late.
MERVYN:	'86? Good Heavens!
COMPERE:	So at the end of the round, Balsover still well ahead, but . . . plenty of time for that to change. For Round Four we go back to the buzzers; first one to press with the correct answer gets the two points. But if you interrupt me too soon and get it wrong, of course it's passed over to the other team, who can themselves score two points, provided of course that the answer is correct. So, lots of points to be won; fingers on buzzers. Question 24: what was the name of the car that held the world land speed record in . . . 19 . . .25? (BUZZER) Bill Wright for Balsover?
BILL:	The Golden Arrow, would it have been?
COMPERE:	No, that wasn't until quite a bit later. Anybody on the Malvern side? No conferring. . . . Have to hurry you. (BUZZER) Malcolm?
MALCOLM:	The Sunbeam?
COMPERE:	Got it in the nick of time. Well done. Question 25: what was F. H. Royce's job before he . . .? (BUZZER) Mervyn Johns for the Mounties?
MERVYN:	Oh sorry, I didn't mean to . . .
COMPERE:	I'm sorry, Mervyn. You've buzzed; I'll have to ask you for an answer.
MERVYN:	Oh er . . . I don't know . . . a mechanic?
COMPERE:	No. Over to the other side: what was F. H. Royce's job before he went into cars? Can anyone come in? (BUZZER)
BOB:	Wasn't he a crane manufacturer? Something to do with cranes?
COMPERE:	Are you asking me or telling me?
BOB:	I think he was a crane manufacturer.
COMPERE:	And you're quite correct – a couple more points to the Fliers. Here's question 26 coming up. Fingers on buzzers again. Similar question. What was Charlie Rolls' father? (2 BUZZERS) Mounties, you were there first. Mervyn?
MERVYN:	He was a lord.
COMPERE:	Quite right. Rolls was in fact from an aristocratic background. And on to the last question of this round. What was the name of the first model of Cadillac to be manufactured? (*pause*) Nobody? (*pause*) (BUZZER) Malcolm of the Mounties?
MALCOLM:	A?
COMPERE:	Yes! Trick question, I suppose, but well done, you get your four points for that. And so the score at the end of Round Four stands at Balsover Fliers 16 Malvern . . .
TUTOR:	Now listen again and check your answers.
TUTOR:	And that's the end of Practice Exam Three.

Exam Four Paper 4

TUTOR: Practice Exam Four. Paper 4: Listening Comprehension. To hear each part again, rewind to the beginning. Look at page 66, questions 1 to 10. You're going to hear a travel guide talking to a group of holidaymakers on a boat trip. It's part of a day-long guided tour. But first read the questions.

Now listen and tick whether the statements are true or false, according to what you hear. Ready?

GUIDE: Now I shouldn't sit too close to the side there. It may look quite calm, but out there in the middle we're liable to meet quite a swell . . . don't want to get our nice smart dresses splashed, do we? Only the other week, a young lad was all but swept out to sea just over there and some time ago, I'm afraid, an older couple weren't so lucky. So, better safe than sorry. Right, well, there it is. That's where we're going. As I was saying before, the island has had quite a chequered history, but now just about half of it is a nature reserve run by the Dorset Naturalists' Trust.

YOUTH: How big is it?
GUIDE: I beg your pardon?
YOUTH: How big is the island?
GUIDE: Well, it's pretty much what you can see from here. It's quite a regular-shaped island, just about round, then tapering off to that headland over there to the west.
YOUTH: Yes, but I mean, er, how big is it in acres?
GUIDE: Ah. . . . Well, it says here that it's just over 500 acres. Incidentally, that's about 200 hectares, give or take the odd square metre. All right? As I was saying, just about all of the island is covered by heathland and woodland, and I'm sure you'll find the whole experience enchanting. If you keep your eyes open this afternoon, you'll see more ducks, geese and wading birds – in the shallow waters round the island – than you're likely to see for the rest of the year. Now we'll be going on a tour that takes about an hour and a half, and that'll take us over . . .
GIRL: Can't we just go off on our own?
YOUTH: Yeh.
GUIDE: If you choose not to come on the guided tour, which for visitors normally costs 60p and we have succeeded in arranging free of charge, we'll meet back at the landing stage at 4.30 sharp. Please don't be late, or else we'll have difficulty in getting to our next port of call before sunset. The hold-up after our pub lunch was really rather unnecessary. Anyway, here we are in the middle now of one of the two largest natural harbours in the world.

AMERICAN: Excuse me. Is this bigger than Sydney harbour or . . .
GUIDE: Er, that is er still being argued about. Er, on your left there you can see Shell Bay stretching round to the famous Old Harry Rocks in the distance. And there's the ferry coming back this way; that goes backwards and forwards all day long over that short stretch of water between the two long beaches. This one, in fact – the Floating Bridge, it's called – is the third of its kind to ply these waters and was built in the late fifties.
JAPANESE: What's that big building on the island?
GUIDE: Ah, that's the castle.
YOUTH: What sort of castle is that, then?
GUIDE: Er, it has no particular historical interest.
GIRL: Can we go in and have a look?
GUIDE: Regrettably it's been closed to the public for some time now.
YOUTH: Typical.
GUIDE: On your left there, you can see an island which is likely to become a household name in the next few years. Apparently there's a reservoir of oil underneath it and there are plans to make it the largest on-shore drilling centre in Europe. As you can imagine, it's not what conservationists would have chosen for the harbour, but . . . there it is. Anyway, we'll soon be disembarking . . .

TUTOR: Now listen again and check your answers.
That's the end of the first part of the test.

TUTOR: **Second part.** Look at questions 11, 12 and 13 on page 66. You're going to hear part of a live talk on the care and repair of antiques. But first read the questions.

Now listen and tick one of the boxes – A, B, C or D – for questions 11, 12 and 13. Ready?

83

SPEAKER: ...Now so far I've been talking about the problems of repairing and restoring antiques of various kinds – pottery, furniture, glass and so on. But breakages are not the only thing that can befall old articles. There is the problem of stains – stains in old wine glasses, coffee stains on tables, stains in cups and vases and such like.

So I thought it would be worth spending some time giving you some general hints on removing stains. And firstly I want to begin with textiles, and by textiles here I mean upholstery, costumes, dolls' dresses, table linen, and carpets and rugs. You can probably immediately think of a dozen things that might stain that Persian rug you've got on the floor, or that table-cloth that belonged to your great-great-grandmother. And I obviously can't deal with all of them. But here are just a few tips. Oh, just a few general words before I talk about different stains. Whenever water is suggested to solve the problem, use distilled water, especially for valuable pieces. Whenever bleaches and other liquids are suggested as a remedy, try them out in a very weak form first. And don't forget to put either a piece of blotting paper, a clean white rag or a pad of paper tissues under the stain before you begin work. And don't be impatient. Some stains need a lot of patience to remove them satisfactorily.

TUTOR: Now listen again and check your answers.
That's the end of the second part of the test.

TUTOR: **Third part**. Look at page 67, questions 14 to 18. You're going to hear a continuation of the talk on the care and repair of antiques. But first read questions 14 to 18.

Now listen and write in the missing information for questions 14 to 18. Ready?

SPEAKER: ...Some stains need a lot of patience to remove them satisfactorily. One of the worst, and unfortunately one of the most common, is milk. You'll know if you've ever left any spilt milk how rancid and smelly it soon goes. But a quick wipe over with a damp rag is not enough. I suggest washing the whole area with warm soapy water – that's usually enough if done quickly. But if the stain persists, wash again, this time adding borax. Another method is to start with white spirit. Or if a stain persists on white cloth, a small amount of gentle bleach can be used quite safely.

Another common stain, of course, is tea or coffee. If recent, both can be removed by putting the fabric over the top of a jug and pouring really hot water through the material from a height.

In the case of coffee, any old obstinate stains can be rubbed with glycerine and left for an hour or so, then rinsed and washed with warm soapy water. On the other hand, coffee spots will often come out if you put blotting paper on both sides and then give it a quick touch with a hot iron. Strangely, that's not recommended for tea stains. You can usually remove dried tea stains with a weak solution of borax – and then rinse out as usual.

Blotting paper, by the way, can also be used to remove candle wax. Put it both sides of the wax stain (or you could use brown wrapping paper) and apply a reasonably hot iron. You just go on replacing the blotting paper (or wrapping paper) until the stain has almost disappeared, and then remove any final traces with white spirit.

A question I'm often asked is how to remove chewing-gum from textiles. Horrible stuff, isn't it? Well, there are two solutions. The first is to work egg white into the gum so that you can pick most of it off and then sponge the remainder off with warm soapy water. The other method is to chill the area with ice and then pick the bits off, washing away the remainder as before. Not too difficult, in fact, but as with all these remedies, have patience. Perhaps just one more before I pause for any questions. Shoe polish. Quite a common problem with rugs and carpets of course, and the solution is fairly easy. Just rub the area with some cotton wool moistened with a small amount of white spirit. It rarely fails – but again remember to

TUTOR: use a very small amount of white spirit and take it steady. Now before I turn to stains on furniture, you might have some stain . . .

TUTOR: Now listen again and check your answers.
That's the end of the third part of the test.

TUTOR: **Fourth part**. Look at questions 19 to 23 on page 68. You're going to hear part of a television studio discussion in front of an invited audience. But first read the questions.

SHEILA: Now listen and tick one of the boxes – A, B, C or D – for questions 19 to 23. Ready? But you see, quite typically, the Right Honourable Gentleman has again answered the wrong question. The questioner in the audience was not asking us to discuss American influence generally, the pros and cons of drinking coca-cola etc., but a much more specific point that has nothing to do with baseball er the English language, or whatever. And I sympathise with the sentiments in the terms of the question. Yes, we have allowed ourselves as a country, indeed as a continent, to become prey to any whim that is felt on the other side of the Atlantic. Our er . . .

WATKINS: If I could come back in here, I . . .
SHEILA: Please let me finish. Our er . . . Take our interest rates, for example; they yo-yo up and down as a result of a falling, stabilising, falling pound, which reflects hardly at all on our own performance in world markets. What Washington wants, Washington gets, and it must be pretty obvious that time and time again our economy – and indeed our people – are the losers. Now my learned colleague points out that the USA is our major ally, . . .
WATKINS: We haven't got a better one, . . .
SHEILA: But an ally in what, I ask myself. In the suppression of other countries' freedom?
WATKINS: Oh come on!
SHEILA: In the race for total domination through nuclear arms superiority?
WATKINS: You're living on another planet.
SHEILA: That's rich, coming from you.
COMPERE: Lord Watkins?
WATKINS: Thank you. You see, Sheila, bless her heart, is viewing things from the traditional insular standpoint that has been responsible . . .
SHEILA: Me, insular? I like that!
WATKINS: . . . that has been responsible for most of our problems over the past few decades. Of course we want freedom. Of course we all want independence, self-determination, but . . . and this is the big 'but' . . . Sheila and her party had better wake up to the fact that no country, no country – be it big or small, powerful or weak – no country can exist today in isolation, friendless and entirely inward-looking.
SHEILA: This is not my point at all. My party, as you will have read, have laid out a three-point plan to resist the trend, to stop us being swallowed up and becoming the 50th – or is it the 51st? – state of America. One: the removal of all American missile bases in the UK. Two: a clear condemnation of any acts of aggression or oppression undertaken in foreign parts by the US government. And three: import controls on all American goods coming into this country until such time as we detect a clear change of policy on the part of their administration.
WATKINS: Now that, if I may say so, is a typical, vote-catching statement by a party – and it sounds like a very desperate party – in Opposition. No responsible government . . .
SHEILA: Would that we had one.
WATKINS: No responsible government would entertain such a recipe for disaster. The effect on our trade alone would be catastrophic. And as for the question of defence, . . .

TUTOR: Now listen again and check your answers.
That's the end of the fourth part of the test.

TUTOR: **Fifth part**. Look at questions 24 to 28 on page 69. You're going to hear a scene from a television drama serial about an American family. The characters are two brothers, Ronald and Bobby, and Ronald's English wife, Kate. But first read the questions.

Now listen and tick one of the boxes – A, B, C or D – for questions 24 to 28. Ready?
RONALD: Why didn't you contact me, Bobby? I should have been here.

BOBBY: I didn't know where you were.
RONALD: You had an address, for God's sake.... I should have been here.
BOBBY: You couldn't have done anything.
RONALD: But to pay my last respects. I mean, ...
BOBBY: Respects?
RONALD: Look, what's got into you, Bobby? Something's eating you; now what is it?
BOBBY: You remember when it was his birthday one year? You must have been thirteen or thereabouts. And I spent every cent I had on a pipe for him. Every cent. And do you remember what you gave him?
RONALD: Bobby.
BOBBY: I said, do you remember what you gave him?
RONALD: A poem.
BOBBY: Yeah, a poem. Some drivel you'd knocked off in a couple of minutes, you with your ...
RONALD: I copied it out of a book.
BOBBY: I guessed you had. And he was all over you. What a great idea for a birthday present! And how he'd never forget ...
RONALD: Bobby!
BOBBY: Such a talent in the family! ... You know what he did with my pipe?
RONALD: I ... I ...
BOBBY: He never once put it to his lips; you know that?
KATE: You can't blame Ronald for that, Bobby.
BOBBY: Who said anything about blame? Am I blaming him? Am I blaming my own dear brother just because my whole goddam life has turned into a ... an empty hole ...?
RONALD: Now steady on, Bobby. Don't take it out on Kate. It's nothing to do with her.
BOBBY: It's got everything to do with her! She's family, isn't she? The English rose, who got the five-star seal of approval from Daddy the moment she opened her goddam mouth.
RONALD: Now look! ...
KATE: It's all right, Ronald. Let it go.
BOBBY: Do you remember when I brought Julie back here, the first and only time. And Daddy hardly said a word to her all evening; just sat there puffing on his pipe and ... God, I loved that girl, Ronny. I ... And when she'd gone, he just said 'Is that the best you can do?'
RONALD: I don't think he meant ...
BOBBY: And you! You and her! 'Like the daughter I never had!' How can you compete with things like that? How could I ...? I could have been somebody, Ronny. I could have been a big man. I wasn't stupid.
RONALD: You were very bright. You are ...
BOBBY: Don't patronise me! The two of you, you and him, and then her, you just destroyed ... whatever there was inside me. I'm like a shell.
KATE: Look, if you're going to sit here wallowing in self-pity all evening, we'd ...
BOBBY: That's right! You go. I don't want you here. You don't belong here. If you'd seen him towards the end ... He used to sit here in the evenings, making goddam excuses for you. 'He's a very busy man!' 'It's a long way to come.' 'The children probably kept them occupied.' It was pathetic! Every now and again he'd come out with something like that, and then ... drift back to his private thoughts, his own little world. So why don't you get back to your smart apartment and your two perfect kids and let Ronny, Mr Success, push through a few more million-dollar deals, and ... and just leave me alone!
RONALD: I loved him too, Bobby.
KATE: You had your chances, Bobby! You just didn't have what it takes. You didn't have to be a 24-carat failure, you know. If you'd ...
BOBBY: Get her out of here! Take what you want. Have the furniture! Take the lot! But just get out, both of you! Just get out. Please.

TUTOR: Now listen again and check your answers.
And that's the end of Practice Exam Four.